GRAHAM HILL

By SIMON ARRON

PHOTOGRAPHS BY

DAVE FRIEDMAN

LAT PHOTOGRAPHIC

DAVID PHIPPS

HAZLETON PUBLISHING

PUBLISHER
Richard Poulter

EXECUTIVE PUBLISHER
Elizabeth Le Breton

ART EDITOR
Steve Small

PRODUCTION MANAGER
George Greenfield

HOUSE EDITOR
Peter Lovering

PRODUCTION ASSISTANT
Deirdre Fenney

STATISTICS
Steve Small

All colour photography is by David Phipps.

Black and white photography by:
David Phipps, Dave Friedman and LAT Photographic.

This first edition published in 1992 by
Hazleton Publishing, 3 Richmond Hill, Richmond,
Surrey TW10 6RE.

ISBN: 0-905138-86-4

Printed in Singapore by Stan Graphics.

Typesetting by First impression Ltd, Richmond, Surrey.

DISTRIBUTORS

UK & OTHER MARKETS
George Philip Ltd, 59 Grosvenor Street
London W1X 9DA

USA & CANADA
Motorbooks International, PO Box 2
729 Prospect Avenue, Osceola
Wisconsin 54020, USA

PROLOGUE

On the evening of Saturday, 29 November 1975, I was listening, surreptitiously, via a cheap plastic earpiece, to Radio Luxembourg's evening rock show. A late-evening news bulletin mentioned a light plane crash somewhere down south. That in itself didn't cause much alarm. When, half an hour later, the item was repeated, it was rumoured that the aircraft in question had belonged to Graham Hill. I remained glued to the radio for the next couple of hours, hoping against hope that there had been some mistake, that somebody else might have borrowed it . . .

The following morning brought grim confirmation. The only man to have won motor racing's unofficial Triple Crown (the Formula 1 World Championship, Indianapolis 500 and Le Mans 24 Hours), the man with more Grand Prix starts to his credit than anyone else in history (a record that would stand until 1989), the man who had only recently retired from the hurly-burly of F1 race driving to concentrate on the fledgling team which carried his own name had perished, along with five other members of his organisation, one of Britain's most promising young talents among them.

With Graham Hill's passing, British motor racing had lost one of its finest ambassadors.

There was a peculiar irony in the manner of his death. During the 20 years that he was an active participant in a wide variety of motor sporting disciplines, including the occasional rally, he only suffered one bad crash, though for most of his career the mortality rate among drivers was alarmingly high.

At the time of the accident, he and his team were on their way back from Paul Ricard in southern France, where they had been testing in preparation for the 1976 season, the start of which was less than two months away. In Tony Brise, Hill had found the ideal driver around whom to develop his own team. Until his plane hit some trees on the edge of Elstree golf course that foggy November evening, the future – even in retirement – looked bright.

The victory that wasn't? Savouring the spoils at Indy in 1966. Hill's triumph was protested by Lotus, who reckoned that USAC's lap scorers had miscounted. Jim Clark attempted to enter Victory Lane, but found that his rival was already celebrating. After much debate, Hill's win was finally confirmed on the Tuesday after the race.

The tossing of a motoring magazine across the factory floor at Smiths Instruments in Cricklewood is not the recognised manner for getting a racing career off the ground, but that's how fate selected Graham Hill for the job.

'Originally, Graham was never all that interested in cars or racing,' recalls Bette, his widow. 'There always seemed to be motor bikes involved in his life, but never cars. Even when he was younger, photographs of him with his parents always seemed to have a bike in the background somewhere.' Indeed, he had a slightly bandy gait as the result of a motor cycle accident that shortened his left leg by half an inch. His father never owned a car, and Graham didn't start driving until he was 24. Bear in mind that, nowadays, a 24-year-old racing driver will probably have accumulated at least ten years' experience in karting and the various junior racing formulae that proliferate. Graham had taken part in some motor bike scrambles, and was also – less relevantly – something of a dab hand at rowing. Throughout his career, his crash helmet bore the colours of the London Rowing Club, to which he belonged. He felt that the discipline and determination that the sport had instilled in him were of great value when he later applied himself to car racing.

Hill, who had shown an early flair for things mechanical, was not happy at Smiths. 'He really didn't *know* what he wanted to do with his life,' remembers Bette.

The magazine that an elder colleague passed to him offered the chance to drive around Brands Hatch for five shillings per lap. Using an imaginary dental appointment as an excuse, he bunked off work one Wednesday and invested one pound in four laps in a Cooper-JAP 500 cc F3 car.

That was enough. He now knew what he wanted to do with his life.

Early in 1954, Graham gave up his regular pay packet at Smiths (without bothering to pass the information on to his father) in order to pursue his motor racing ambitions. He signed on the dole, giving his profession as 'racing driver', but with no such vacancies forthcoming that somewhat limited source of income dried up after a few months.

Thus he had precious little cash and – after his first car, an extremely ropey Morris 8, had been written off when it was T-boned by a laundry van – only a bicycle for transport. 'Courting', says Bette, 'was a bit difficult. He lived in Maida Vale, me in Catford and he was working, unpaid, as a mechanic in Westerham. The deal was that he would prepare cars for people in exchange for the odd drive.' Bette was working for Automotive Products, and at least earned something, but times were tough – though interesting.

*The young Hill's sporting prowess was apparent
on water, as a member of the London Rowing Club,
whose colours he carried on his crash helmet
throughout his career.*

*Early days: Hill began his career by offering his
mechanical services in exchange for drives. Here he gets
to grips with a 500 cc Kieft at Brands Hatch.*

Hill's mechanical endeavours finally brought their reward on 27 April 1954, when he took the wheel of a Mk IV Cooper-JAP in a Formula 3 race at Brands Hatch. Although for ever labelled as a driver who achieved results through determination rather than ability, the fact that he qualified on the front row for his heat indicated that he had more than a little natural aptitude.

Curiously, it wasn't only the first race in which he had participated. It was also the first he had ever attended! Although he had been a regular visitor to Brands, he had previously only been there on racing school and test days.

Graham tore off the line into the lead, 'but I think he was so surprised himself that they all shot past him before long,' recalls Bette, who was watching from the roof of a friend's car. 'The amazing thing was that he knew just so little about the sport then. He really wasn't sure what to do.'

All the same, he eventually finished second and took fourth place in the final. He was lying second in his next event when an engine problem forced him out.

At this time, he had suggested to the chap for whom he was preparing cars that it might be a reasonable time to think about some sort of salary. The car owner disagreed, which left Hill – after this particular event – wandering around Brands Hatch with no obvious means of getting back to London.

He cadged a ride in a furniture lorry which doubled as a transporter, the driver of which turned out to be Colin Chapman, the now legendary founder of Lotus Cars. In those days, Lotus was based under the arches in Hornsey, north London, rather than in the glamorous latter-day surroundings of Ketteringham Hall. Over a cup of tea on the return journey, Hill offered his services to Chapman who took him on, part-time, for one pound per day.

In 1955, Hill continued to do odd jobs here and there. One of them, again unpaid, saw him working for Dan Margulies, for whom he acted as riding mechanic in a Sardinian road race. Later, Margulies offered him a shared drive in the Messina 10 Hours, at the helm of the former's Jaguar C-type. It was the first time that Hill's name appeared on an entry list alongside established, world-class opposition such as Mike Hawthorn and Eugenio Castelotti.

The car's proprietor crashed out of the event, and Graham returned, courtesy of an early forerunner of the British Rail Supersaver ticket, to England, where he and Bette were due to tie the knot. Their honeymoon centred on Bognor, conveniently close to Goodwood . . . where Team Lotus had nominated him as reserve driver for a sports car event, though his services ultimately weren't required.

*In order to keep a vital date with Bette, Graham had to
take the train from Messina, in Sicily, where he had
been scheduled to co-drive Dan Margulies's Jaguar
C-type in a ten-hour road race.*

To cope with the extra financial burden of marriage, Graham accepted a full-time position at Lotus, as a result of which his career was to take off for real.

After Hill had cajoled a rather infrequent series of bits and pieces races for the best part of two seasons, during which he won one minor event at Blandford, Chapman offered him a deal for 1956. He made available a kit of Lotus XI parts, which remained Chapman's property but which Hill was free to use so long as he prepared and raced the car in his own time.

Finished in a fairly violent shade of canary, it was known, predictably enough, as the 'Yellow Peril'. Concentrating upon the *Autosport* Championship, he could have taken the title but for a con rod failure during the series' finale at Oulton Park.

In all, Hill won four races, and also notched up six other top-three results in a season that saw him dovetail his numerous Lotus commitments (he also drove cars for Tommy Sopwith and J.J. Richards) with occasional outings in Equipe Endeavour's Cooper-Climax. It wasn't all plain sailing, however. During one particularly wet event at Brands Hatch, he was black-flagged for spinning four times in as many laps, an event Bette remembers well. 'His face was like thunder afterwards. The Clerk of the Course felt there must be something wrong with the car, but it was just Graham trying too hard.'

In June, he paid his first visit to Le Mans. As the team's reserve-cum-mechanic, however, he took no part in the race itself.

Hill's progress at Lotus was such that Chapman wasn't keen to repeat the offer of a car for the 1957 season. As he was now responsible for Lotus's gearbox division, he was too useful to the company to be letting motor racing commitments interfere with what the Lotus boss saw as his main responsibility.

In order to continue with his racing ambitions, Graham thus had to reacquaint himself with the art of wangling drives where he could. By now, however, he at least had the benefit of some solid results under his belt. Offers were plentiful, and he was even *paid* to race for the first time. Given the rather uncertain state of his bank balance to that point, this started to make an already irresistible challenge even more appealing.

Hill raced a variety of privately entered Lotuses and Aston Martins (including Tommy Atkins's DB3S) during the season, taking a handful of wins. He had his first major single-seater race on Easter Monday at Goodwood, where he stalled at the start and finished a solid last.

Towards the end of the year, he finished second at Brands Hatch in John Willment's

*The 1958 Italian Grand Prix at Monza gave Hill his
first GP finish, but in those days sixth place was not
enough to earn him a World Championship point.*

eponymous 1500 cc sports racer. With no prospect of a factory drive from his then employer, he was attracted by Willment's offer of a regular Formula 2 drive in a new chassis that was in the process of evolution. Colin Chapman realised that he was about to lose Hill's services, and promptly offered him a racing deal, but Graham was by then committed to the Willment project.

Ultimately, the Willment F2 was stillborn. When it failed to materialise, Willment put in a good word for Hill with John Cooper, who entered him briefly as number three to Jack Brabham and Roy Salvadori in his F2 team. With his moral obligation to Willment effectively over, however, Hill was happy to accept a fresh proposal from Chapman, which took him back to Lotus as a works driver for a couple of races at the end of '57 and the whole of 1958.

This time, the programme was more substantial. Hill's stock was rather greater than it had been a couple of years earlier, when he had built up his own Lotus XI. This time, he was to be taken on for his driving ability, rather than his mechanical prowess. He was an integral part of Team Lotus's F1 plans.

As number two to Cliff Allison, he made his Grand Prix debut at Monaco on 18 May, less than four years after his first tentative laps in that F3 race at Brands Hatch. At that point, his whole career encompassed about 40 races.

Although not quite as skint as they had been, Bette and Graham still couldn't afford the air fare. The Lotus Mk XIIs travelled down in a furniture truck, the Hills in an unlikely predecessor to the modern GP driver's Lear Jet – an Austin A35.

Bette: 'We were very green. To us it was a big adventure. The people we were mixing with, Hawthorn, Moss and so on, were heroes to me, yet they made us feel very welcome, very much as though we were a part of that world. The atmosphere and the camaraderie were incredible.'

Hill qualified on the back row, and worked his way up to fourth place without actually overtaking anybody, such was the rate of attrition. Eventually, he lost a rear wheel following a halfshaft failure, which set the pattern for a frustrating first season.

After being treated for exhaustion, he set off for the celebrated local casino with Chapman, where they proceeded to 'invest' their start money, which had originally been meant to cover hotel bills and fuel for the return trip. To the considerable relief of their respective spouses, Jack Brabham arrived at an opportune moment and dragged them away from the tables, happily while they were ahead.

Engine failures put Hill out at Zandvoort and Spa, and there followed an alarming moment at Reims – the only time he competed in the same race as the great Juan-Manuel Fangio – when his new Lotus 16's oil filler cap popped off and coated his thigh

*Boxing Day, 1958. The determined Hill saw off the
fancied hordes of Lotus XIs with his works-entered
Seven.*

in scalding fluid, causing him to start clambering out while still travelling at speed.

It wasn't until his eighth Grand Prix, the Italian at Monza, that Graham finally recorded his first finish, taking sixth place (at a time when championship points were awarded only to the top five). He also went the distance in the seasonal finale, the Moroccan Grand Prix at Casablanca, albeit in 16th place.

All in all, the F1 season was plagued by unreliability. Lotus scored only three World Championship points (earned by Allison in Belgium), although the factory's sports car programme produced a few victories on home soil. At Le Mans, where Graham was actually competing for the first time, he and Allison shared a two-litre Mk XV but retired with overheating.

In addition to his busy racing schedule, which also included a few F2 races for the works team in 1958, Hill now had business interests away from the track, though Speedwell Conversions' activities were fairly closely related to their co-founder's (Hill was one of four partners) main occupation.

Speedwell specialised in aftermarket performance conversions. To endorse his own product, Hill – who would prove to be an accomplished touring car racer throughout his career – enjoyed some success in a Speedwell-tuned Austin A35. It's perhaps as well that the authorities were more tolerant of pranks in those days, as Hill admitted a few years later to having run a Speedwell Mini on nitro-methane in one event. Eyebrows were raised when the tiny BMC device blitzed past a 3.8 Jaguar . . . down the straight. Unsurprisingly, the engine blew up long before any post-race explanations were necessary.

Apart from the A35, 1959 was spent at the wheel of myriad works Lotuses, the F1 World Championship season once again being squeezed in between ever busier Formula 2 and sports car commitments. For Hill, it was a disappointing year, his only victories coming in sports cars. Lotus's new recruit Innes Ireland bagged five World Championship points, but Graham drew a blank once more. He was seventh in the Dutch GP (a good drive after losing a lap early on), and ninth on home soil at Aintree. He failed to finish all his other Grands Prix, fifth places in the non-championship Aintree 200 and Oulton Park Gold Cup providing only small crumbs of comfort.

Graham's F2 campaign was similarly blighted by unreliability. When BRM, for whom Jo Bonnier had scored a maiden World Championship victory at Zandvoort, offered him a place in its F1 team alongside Bonnier and Dan Gurney for 1960, he was happy to take up the invitation. An improved financial package was part of the deal; with an infant daughter, Brigitte, to consider, and a second child on the way, it all made perfect sense.

Lotus didn't think so. Chapman showed Hill drawings of his forthcoming rear-engined chassis (a concept first seen the previous season, when it proved to be devastatingly effective, Jack Brabham taking the first of two consecutive world titles for Cooper) in a bid to convince him to stay.

That didn't work, nor did the injunction which Lotus slapped on their former asset to try and prevent his taking part in the Argentine Grand Prix which opened the season in February. Eventually it was all resolved amicably, and Hill embarked upon a long career with BRM.

Ironically, Lotus's fortunes took a major upturn over the course of the next 12 months, Chapman's troops picking up a total of 37 points to BRM's eight.

At the start of the season, BRM swapped and changed between its front- and rear-engined designs. Hill's first race ended disappointingly with a dropped valve spring, and at Monaco he crashed into the timekeepers' box. He finally scored his first championship points at Zandvoort, hanging on to third place by just one second from a charging Stirling Moss.

The balance of the Grand Prix season bore an uncanny similarity to those which had gone before, but there were signs of real promise. In the French GP at Reims, Hill qualified on the front row for the first time in his Grand Prix career, only to encounter a clutch problem at the start. After stalling, he was clobbered by Maurice Trintignant's Aston and retired on the spot.

The next World Championship event, two weeks later at Silverstone, started in similar fashion. Having wasted his front row qualification by stalling, Hill received a glancing blow from Tony Brooks's Cooper before being push-started away, by now firmly last.

In one of the most memorable drives of his career, Hill scythed through the 24-car field, working his way up into second place by half-distance. He chipped away at Jack Brabham's advantage and, on lap 55 of 77, swept past into an improbable lead. Brabham hung on to the BRM's tail, and profited when Hill's efforts began to take their toll on the BRM's brakes. As the leading pair came upon a couple of slower cars on the run down to Copse, Hill opted to try and get past both before the corner, in a determined effort to shake off the dogged Australian. Seconds later he was walking back to the pits, to a massive ovation from the crowd, having learned that his brakes were no longer up to the job of braking quite *that* late, the BRM spinning into retirement. It was as close as he would ever come to winning his home Grand Prix, an omission from his CV which he deeply regretted.

The Portuguese GP culminated in gearbox failure, the American in a blown engine, but Graham was classified in the World Championship for the very first time, his Dutch GP result earning him joint 15th place.

In 1961, Hill finished only three Grands Prix. He
collected his first point of the season at Reims, where he
leads Ireland, Clark, Bonnier, eventual winner – and
World Championship debutant! – Baghetti and
McLaren early in the race.

*Flying start: Hill gave the E-type Jaguar a winning
competition debut at Oulton Park in April 1961.*

The season's non-championship F1 races brought greater consistency, the best result being a second place in the Silver City Trophy at Brands Hatch. In addition, Hill drove for the works Porsche team in both Formula 2 and sports car events, though these netted no more than a brace of class victories. At Le Mans, he and BRM colleague Bonnier shared an RSK 1600, but succumbed to engine failure.

After sampling the Tasman Championship (a now defunct series of races in the Antipodes, which attracted the world's finest teams and drivers during its heyday) for the first time during the European winter, Hill faced the 1961 season with BRM ill-prepared for the change from the 2.5-litre Formula 1 to its 1.5-litre successor.

His F1 career continued its fragile course. BRM slotted Coventry Climax's 1.5-litre four-cylinder into its old 2.5 chassis, and Hill finished just three of the year's eight events, placing 13th in the World Championship after picking up a fifth place in America and a sixth in France. At the end of the year, BRM ran its V8 for the first time. A practice fire precluded its race debut in Italy, but Hill lay second at Watkins Glen until losing a lap in the pits with magneto trouble. His eventual fifth place and team-mate Tony Brooks's third at least offered hope for 1962.

Away from Grands Prix, Graham's schedule was more varied than ever before. He competed in the Targa Florio for the first time, sharing a Porsche RSK with Stirling Moss until the differential broke. He and Moss were also unsuccessful partners at Sebring (Maserati T61 'Birdcage'), the Nürburgring (Porsche RSK) and Le Mans (Ferrari 250GT).

On a more positive note, there were race victories with Equipe Endeavour's Jaguar 3.8 saloon, and he gave the same team's Jaguar E-type a celebrated victory on the car's race debut at Oulton Park, beating a high-class field which included Jack Sears's Ferrari 250GT and Innes Ireland's Aston Martin DB4.

*At Sebring in 1961, he shared Camoradi's Maserati T61
'Birdcage' with Stirling Moss (in overalls, to immediate
left of cockpit). A broken exhaust manifold forced their
retirement. Just over a year later, Hill was an eye-
witness to the Goodwood accident which ended Moss's
career, an incident which affected Graham profoundly.*

The following year, 1962, started in promising style, with victory in a Scalextric competition at the Racing Car Show . . . Hill also served further notice of his versatility when he took tenth overall on the Monte Carlo Rally, sharing a Sunbeam Rapier with Peter Jopp.

BRM skipped the Tasman Championship in order to concentrate upon developing its Type 57 V8 over the winter. The combination won first time out, in the first heat of the non-championship Brussels GP. A push-start at the start of the second heat led to disqualification, however, so the first outright F1 win had to wait until the Easter meeting at Goodwood.

It had taken Hill as long – and rather more races – to register his maiden F1 victory as it had to break into F1 in the first place. When it finally came, the gloss was removed, and his achievement overshadowed, by the dreadful accident which befell Stirling Moss in the same race. It ended a brilliant racing career, and left a deep impression on Hill, who had been an eye-witness.

His victory in the International Trophy at Silverstone was an altogether more cheerful affair. While he diced with John Surtees's Lola and team-mate Richie Ginther's BRM in the early stages, there was precious little sign of the excitement to come as Jim Clark's Lotus stormed off into the distance. Hill's chances appeared to be further compromised as his V8 sounded ever flatter, the result of a couple of branches of his V8's vertical exhaust stack having fallen off.

As the race wore on, it became apparent that the absence of a couple of exhausts wasn't slowing him down. In wet conditions, he began to grind into Clark's lead. With six laps to go he was still 17 seconds adrift. Now the gap started to shrink massively, but going into the final lap there was still almost five seconds between them. Clark lost vital time lapping Masten Gregory, and as the two leaders came up through Abbey Curve for the final time the BRM was up with the Lotus.

In those days, Woodcote was an awesomely fast, sweeping right-hander. Clark stuck to the drier, inside line to defend his position, but the grimly determined Hill wasn't going to be deterred. His only chance was to try the wetter part of the circuit, around the outside. He hung on amid a flurry of opposite lock, his momentum carrying him past his startled rival so that he crossed the line, still sideways, to take a magnificent victory. The margin? About the width of a potato crisp . . .

The World Championship didn't start until 20 May, in Holland, and Hill confirmed that BRM would be in serious contention for the title, qualifying in the middle of the front row between Surtees and Clark. The latter was at the wheel of Colin Chapman's revolutionary Lotus 25, the very first monocoque-construction Grand Prix racer. At the start, Clark hauled away into the lead before gear selection bothers intervened, leaving Hill to pick up the pieces. After a run of disappointments, BRM patron Sir Alfred Owen had threatened to discontinue the team if it didn't pull up its socks in 1962. He wanted a minimum of two victories, so Hill's run to the chequered flag was a pretty useful start as far as the team's very future was concerned, let alone Graham's championship chances.

'The excitement was incredible,' recalls Bette, who as ever kept a vigil from the pit counter, where she was busy keeping lap times. 'Alan Challis, Graham's mechanic, was having to lip-read the times I was giving to him amid all the noise, but we seemed to manage OK. We were all absolutely elated. It was a magic day, and it felt nice to be a part of it, as wives and girlfriends took a much more active role then.'

That set a pattern for the season in which the World Championship battle between Clark and Hill would only be settled on 29 December in South Africa, at the last of the nine rounds.

At Monaco, Hill led for most of the race, despite failing oil pressure. He was comfortably ahead when, on lap 93 of 100, a con rod popped out through the block. The high casualty rate meant that he was still classified a somewhat disappointed sixth. In Belgium, he took pole position, but was hampered in the race by a misfire. As Clark moved in to score his first World Championship victory, Hill profited from a huge accident between Willy Mairesse and Trevor Taylor (who somehow escaped serious injury after knocking down a telegraph pole) to take second place, moving him back into a clear, though slender, championship lead.

The two rivals were on the front row again in France, where Hill was leading before being tipped into a spin while lapping a back-marker. He rejoined after a precautionary pit stop, retaking the lead before a problem with the fuel injection system dropped him to ninth. Dan Gurney went on to give Porsche its only GP victory to date, while Clark also failed to score.

At last! Hill's first GP win came at Zandvoort in 1962.

Hill leads Clark, Surtees, McLaren, Ireland, Brabham, Maggs, Gurney and the rest at the start of the 1962 French GP. Fuel injection trouble eventually delayed him.

In his own estimation, the 1962 German GP victory was one of the toughest, and most satisfying, of Hill's career. Despite pain from a heavy practice accident the previous day, he held off John Surtees and Dan Gurney in teeming rain. No other race ever demanded quite such fierce concentration.

In Britain, the nimble Lotus proved ideally suited to Aintree, and Clark won at a canter, closing the championship gap to just one point as Hill came home fourth, his BRM wearing out its tyres at oddly differing rates.

Hill had a new car for the German GP, albeit briefly. During practice, the Dutch privateer Carel Godin de Beaufort was lapping with a crude form of on-board camera strapped to the back of his Porsche. The apparatus's mounting points simply weren't up to the task of supporting such a weight, however, and the whole structure collapsed and landed in the centre of the circuit. Enter G. Hill . . .

The BRM ran straight over the unintentionally abandoned camera, perforating its sump. The sudden coating of oil over the rear wheels caused Hill to fly off the road, the slick also catching out Tony Maggs's Cooper before Hill had a chance to warn approaching drivers.

Bruised, Graham started his old car from the front row and went on to win in dismal conditions that actually helped him, for the reduced loads upon the driver meant that the previous day's battering wasn't quite so apparent. Surtees and Gurney applied pressure throughout, but the BRM stayed in front to the end. It was, he later reckoned, the race which had demanded the greatest concentration he had ever known. As for Clark, he was left behind at the start, after forgetting to actuate his fuel pump. After passing no fewer than 17 cars in one lap, he settled back to finish fourth after a couple of lurid moments.

As an indication of how tired he felt, Hill crashed out of a saloon car race at Brands Hatch the following day, hitting his Jaguar's throttle instead of the brake going into Druids. As if the stress of the Nürburgring hadn't been enough, he was contracted to appear at the German GP prize-giving ceremony, which didn't allow him to get back to the UK until the early hours of the morning, permitting only a brief sleep before he went to Brands . . .

In the Italian GP at Monza, Hill led home Ginther in a BRM 1-2. Victory in the American GP would be enough to clinch the title; with a driver's best five scores being taken into account, his four wins and one second would be unbeatable.

It was Clark who triumphed at Watkins Glen, however, by eight seconds from Hill. That meant that a win for Clark in South Africa, almost 12 weeks hence, would give him the title. Hill already had 39 points, but could only add to that by winning the race. If Clark won, he too would have 39 – and would take the crown by dint of four wins to Hill's three.

The long build-up merely added to the tension. Before the race at the East London circuit, there were two non-championship races at Kyalami and Westmead, neither of which brought Hill any joy. Indeed, persistent ignition trouble rather sapped the

The climax to the 1962 season wasn't helped by the hiatus between the US GP and the crunch race in South Africa. Hill and Clark had to wait the best part of three months. Jimmy looked set to pinch the crown from under Graham's nose, but the Lotus's Climax engine proved too fragile, leaving Hill to win both the race and the championship title.

*In the early 1960s, Hill built up an excellent working
relationship with BRM's Tony Rudd (left).*

team's confidence. He also took part in the London-to-Brighton run, an experience
which proved to be rather more frightening than anything he'd encountered in F1 up
to that point, following several mishaps along the way.

Clark and Hill shared the front row for the big showdown, the former on pole by
three-quarters of a second. Predictably, it was the Lotus which speared away into the
lead. The championship appeared to be Jimmy's for the taking, Hill only able to watch
from a distant second place. Then, with 20 laps to go, Clark pitted, the rear of his car
wreathed in smoke. Its Climax engine had broken, and the championship title which
he had looked so close to losing was Graham's, BRM taking the constructors' award
for good measure.

Part of his reward for winning the title was to spend a short spell in a Pakistani gaol,
after a mix-up over vaccination certificates *en route* to contesting some Tasman events
in Rob Walker's four-wheel drive Ferguson.

All in all, it had been a successful year, Hill's first World Championship title complemented by numerous saloon car victories in John Coombs's Jaguar 3.8, some good GT results in the same entrant's E-type and a brief stint in the lead in Aston Martin's experimental 4.0 212 at Le Mans, where he shared with Ginther. There had also been a victory in the Archie Scott-Brown Memorial sports car race at Snetterton, in one of UDT Laystall's Lotus 19s.

The Tasman foray with Walker yielded a second place at Lakeside, and before the F1 season started in earnest he shared third place with Pedro Rodriguez (NART Ferrari 330LM SP) in the Sebring 12 Hours.

Although a blown engine put him out of the 1962 Aintree 200, victory in John Coombs's Jaguar in the supporting touring car event was some consolation.

The BRM P57 was no match for Jim Clark's Lotus 25
in 1963 and Hill spent much of the season battling for
the placings – as in the British Grand Prix, where he
finished third after running out of fuel.

With its intended '63 chassis, the Type 61, not yet ready, the Bourne team continued with the successful Type 57s at the start of the year. It didn't do too much harm. A couple of things had changed at Monaco since the Grand Prix teams' last visit.

One was the location of the startline, moved to its present-day site before Ste Devote, after a marshal had been fatally wounded by wreckage from Ginther's BRM during a first-corner pile-up in '62. Another was Hill's luck.

Having come so close to victory the previous year, Graham profited from Clark's gearbox malady to break his Monégasque duck this time around, leading home another BRM 1-2 as he did so. It was to be the first of five victories around the streets of the Principality, a feat that none of his contemporaries could match.

As far as F1 was concerned, the Monaco victory offered only temporary respite before Clark and Lotus got into their stride. The Scot completely demolished the opposition, going on to win seven of the ten events. Hill nevertheless finished joint second (with Ginther) in the points table, taking the Type 61 to third places at Reims and Silverstone, although he would have been second on home ground had he not run out of fuel.

The team reverted to its older chassis for the final three races of the year, Hill winning at Watkins Glen, despite a broken anti-roll bar. His cause was helped when Surtees's Ferrari obligingly suffered a piston failure while leading. He finished in the points in both Mexico and South Africa, and non-championship victories in the Lombank Trophy, at Snetterton, and the Aintree 200 meant that the season was quite successful, even if Clark had been competing on a different plane.

Although the 1963 F1 season was a relative disappointment after his 1962 world title, the year did have other compensations. One such was victory in the Tourist Trophy at Goodwood, aboard Maranello Concessionaires' Ferrari GTO.

A steady run with the Rover-BRM turbine netted Hill and Ginther seventh place on the road at Le Mans in 1963, although the car wasn't officially classified. The organisers didn't have a suitable class in which to place it . . .

Hill's first experience of Indianapolis came in 1963, with the Mickey Thompson Special. After losing a wheel during a practice run, he decided to give the 500 a miss. For the time being, at least . . .

Hill had paid his first visit to Indianapolis, but withdrew from the race after a wheel came off in qualifying and put him in the wall. He reckoned the handling had been sufficiently spooky on four wheels, and filed Indy away at the back of his mind for another couple of years.

For Le Mans, he had been entrusted with development of the intriguing gas turbine-powered Rover-BRM, which was reckoned to have an idling speed of around 30,000 rpm. Graham shared with Ginther and, starting 30 seconds behind the rest of the field, the two ran reliably into seventh place, though they weren't included in the official results as the organisers didn't really have a suitable class to put them in. There were numerous successes of a more conventional nature in John Coombs's Jaguar fleet, while a Speedwell-modified Sprite was freighted over to contest the Sebring 3 Hours, from which he retired with axle failure.

Under pressure at Mosport Park in 1963, Hill holds off Lloyd Ruby, Roger Penske and Jerry Grant in BRP's Lotus 19. It was all in vain, his Climax engine eventually suffering a holed piston.

As it had in 1962, the World Championship fight went all the way to the final round in 1964. And Hill was once again one of the leading players.

The year started brightly enough. In the Tasman series he drove a Brabham for the very first time, taking Scuderia Veloce's BT3 to victory in his second race for the team, the South Pacific Trophy at Longford. His next task was to tackle the Monte Carlo Rally with the unlikely bulk of a Ford Falcon. In fact one of the giant American saloons finished second overall, but it wasn't Hill's. His was extremely dog-eared by the end, after substantial contact with several stout sections of the Alpine countryside.

BRM's new monocoque design, the 261, was shaken down in a couple of non-championship races early in the year. Or perhaps shaken up would be a better description. At Snetterton, Hill was leading the *Daily Mirror* Trophy when he aquaplaned off the circuit and into the bank.

The 261 continued to show promise elsewhere. He led Goodwood's *News of the World* Trophy until suffering a rotor arm breakage two laps from the end. The Aintree 200 produced a second place, and the International Trophy appeared to be his for the taking when Jack Brabham pulled off a stunt which would have been remarkably familiar to Hill. He passed him at the final corner . . . just as Graham had done to Jim Clark in the corresponding fixture two years earlier.

Despite handling problems, Hill put the new P261 on
pole for the 1964 Aintree 200. After leading initially,
he succumbed to Brabham and Clark, though he
eventually finished second after the Scotsman flew off
the track.

The World Championship season started in earnest at Monaco, where Hill and Ginther repeated their 1-2 success of the previous season. It wasn't all plain sailing, though. Clark's Lotus 25 had taken pole, and had streaked away at the start. Uncharacteristically, he then clipped the barriers at the exit of the chicane, damaging his anti-roll bar mounting. That left a roll bar trailing along the track, but you'd never have known the car was damaged as he continued to increase his lead. ;

Eventually, the Scot pitted to have the debris removed and rejoined just behind Gurney and Hill. Just after half-distance, the BRM moved ahead for the first time. After Gurney's demise, Clark tried all he could to peg back Hill's advantage, but to no avail. Late in the race, his engine gave up and he was classified fourth as Hill motored serenely on to win by a clear lap.

It was a particularly good result for BRM, as Ginther – already swathed in bandages after a big accident at Aintree – completed most of the race without the aid of a gear-lever knob, at a circuit which demands more changes per lap than any other . . .

Clark redressed the balance in Holland. Hill briefly worked his way into second place, but began to drop back with fuel vaporisation. He peeled into the pits where Tony Rudd administered a hi-tech cure: he chucked a bucket of water over the fuel pump, which had been overheating. This smart piece of improvisation worked well enough; Hill rejoined to finish fourth.

At Spa, Clark qualified on pole by two seconds, but in the race neither he nor Hill had any answer to Gurney's Brabham. With a couple of laps to go, Clark pitted with overheating, rejoining in a distant fourth place.

On the final lap, Gurney stuttered to a halt out of fuel, handing Graham what would have been an improbable victory. Then the BRM too ran dry. Gurney and Hill could only watch as Bruce McLaren sped past in his Cooper. McLaren almost made the finishing line before his engine started to cough . . . and into view hove Clark. The Lotus driver gratefully acknowledged the chequered flag before he, too, ran out of fuel on the slowing-down lap. For Hill, the net result was fifth place.

There followed a string of second places. Firstly at Le Mans, where he and Jo Bonnier enjoyed the challenge of taking on the works Ferraris with Col. Ronnie Hoare's privately entered 330P3. One week later, he was second to Gurney in the French GP at Rouen. The British GP moved to Brands Hatch for the first time, the third different circuit in three years. The winner remained the same, though, Clark beating Hill by less than three seconds. In Germany, Graham's V8 developed a misfire, but he finished a distant second to Surtees.

Hill was now leading the championship, so the testing accident he suffered at Snetterton

Hill leads Clark and McLaren during their pursuit of Dan Gurney in the 1964 Belgian GP. All of them eventually ran out of fuel, though the Scot didn't do so until after the chequered flag.

was the last thing he needed. He sustained a chipped bone in his neck, though he was cleared to race with an inflatable surgical collar. Typically, the next World Championship race was at the super-bumpy Zeltweg circuit. With a characteristically stubborn refusal to be beaten by such a setback, he qualified on pole, though a broken distributor drive saved his neck from too much punishment.

Despite his retirement, Graham retained his championship lead, as he did after Monza. In Italy, he qualified third but lost his clutch on the line and went no further. With two races to go, Hill still had two points in hand over Clark, with dark horse Surtees sneaking up on the rails, a further two adrift.

At Watkins Glen, Clark suffered yet another mechanical failure when well ahead, and Hill went on to win from Surtees. All three men could still take the title in Mexico, but the odds favoured Hill, even though he had to finish third or better to improve his points score (a driver could only count his best six results).

The final race got off to a bad start for Hill, whose goggles slipped while he was adjusting the elastic. With gloved hands, he fiddled around and sorted them out, but the race started as he did so and he slipped back to tenth place. Surtees, preferring Ferrari's proven V8 to the quicker but less trustworthy flat-12, was left to contemplate the wisdom of that choice as a misfire set in and left him even further down the field than Hill.

Clark, who needed to win to have any chance, predictably tore off into the lead. Equally predictably, he broke down. This time, it was far more agonising than South Africa in 1962. Despite a split oil pipe, he nursed the car almost to the flag. Only after he'd started his final lap did the engine seize. By that stage of the race, Hill was far enough back that the title would have been Clark's had he made it . . .

Hill had charged into an impressive third place, with Ferrari team-mates Bandini and Surtees just behind. Third place would have been enough for Hill, irrespective of the others' performances, but it was not to be. The impetuous Bandini careered into him at the hairpin after several unsuccessful attempts to pass. The BRM spun round and pitted with crimped exhausts, having impacted lightly with the guard rail.

Even so, Clark's last-lap misfortune was enough to give Hill the title so long as Surtees remained third. The Ferrari team gesticulated wildly to Bandini, by now running second to Gurney, and the Italian got the message. He backed off, and allowed Surtees to snatch a title that only a couple of minutes earlier had looked destined for Clark, and had passed briefly within Hill's grasp before Ferrari team orders altered the verdict. Hill finished the year with a total of 41 points to Surtees's 40, but under the dropped scores rule he could count only 39 of them . . .

Dickie Attwood hassles Hill's Brabham-BMW during the 1965 London Trophy. The latter finished second in both heats at Crystal Palace, and was beaten on aggregate by Jim Clark – who had jetted back from Indianapolis to compete. Clark had won in the States, too.

For the second season running, Hill was second in the drivers' World Championship, and once again he had proved his versatility. In addition to the second place at Le Mans, there were several victories in GT, touring car and sports car events, most pleasurably a defeat of the works Ferraris in the Reims 12 Hours, when he and Bonnier teamed up once again in Col. Ronnie Hoare's 250LM. He also hung on grimly to take second place in the London Trophy F2 meeting at Crystal Palace. At the wheel of John Coombs's Cooper, handling a bit like a supermarket trolley on ice with a broken roll bar, he and the other established stars were put firmly in their place by a then unknown Austrian by the name of Rindt.

The dominance of British drivers in the World Championship continued in 1965, when Hill – who also had a busy F2 schedule with John Coombs, not to mention miscellaneous sports car rides and a third child, Samantha – had a new partner at BRM in the form of the youthful Jackie Stewart, with whom he would also share the latest evolution of the Rover-BRM turbine car at Le Mans (where the utterly reliable device came in tenth). The Scottish rookie finished sixth first time out in South Africa, where Hill trailed home third behind familiar adversaries Clark and Surtees.

His chances of completing a Monte Carlo hat-trick were enhanced by the absence of Clark, who was otherwise engaged at Indianapolis (where, like most things he turned

Hill drove John Coombs's Oldsmobile-powered McLaren-Elva on several occasions in 1965. Here at Riverside, he retired from the Times GP when the car shed a wheel.

his hand to in 1965, he won). Sure enough, Hill qualified on pole and was soon pulling away from everyone bar Stewart. On lap 25, his comfortable Sunday afternoon drive was rudely interrupted.

He suddenly came across Bob Anderson's Brabham trickling down the centre of the road, jammed in first gear. With no warning flags to alert him of the impending danger, it was as much as Graham could do to skate up the chicane escape road, where he pulled up with his engine stalled.

Determination intact, he hopped out, manhandled the car around so that it was facing back down the escape road, jumped in and successfully managed to bump-start the V8 back into life. He rejoined the circuit over half a minute behind Stewart and the Ferraris of Bandini and Surtees. The BRM newcomer spun shortly afterwards, handing the lead to Bandini. But Brabham was closing fast, though his stint in front was curtailed by failing oil pressure.

Hill was looming up fast, and by half-distance he was with the two Italian machines. Surtees capitulated fairly quickly, but it wasn't until lap 65 that Bandini succumbed to the press-on Englishman. Although the leading Ferrari hung on for a few laps, Hill eventually pulled away to win by over a minute. It had been a magnificent effort, during which he posted a fastest lap 0.8 seconds quicker than his pole-position time.

Thereafter he was to enjoy a remarkably consistent season, though there would be only one further victory. After Monaco, he finished every race in the points until the final Grand Prix in Mexico, where he posted his only retirement of the season. The problem was Clark, whose absence at Monaco hardly compromised his championship hopes. He returned to F1 at Spa and went on to win the next five races . . .

Hill qualified on pole by almost two seconds in Belgium, but erred on set-up and finished fifth. After a hefty practice accident at Clermont- Ferrand, which was hosting the French GP for the first time, it was a rather battered Hill who finished fifth. At Silverstone, he was second – by three seconds – to Clark, having had to pump his brakes for most of the race. After the Dutch GP, where he finished fourth, a long way behind Clark, the World Championship was all but settled in the Scotsman's favour. There was still a mathematical chance of his overhauling Clark's tally, if you believed in fairies. Then Clark won – from Hill – in Germany, and the issue was put beyond doubt.

BRM returned to the winners' circle at Monza when Clark suffered a broken fuel pump. But Hill was second once again, as Stewart scored the first of his 27 World Championship victories. Leading under pressure from his young team-mate, the elder partner ran wide briefly and that gave Stewart the break he needed.

Privately, Hill was angry that the team hadn't ordered Stewart to hold station behind him, though he was mollified by a third consecutive victory at Watkins Glen. It was to be his last Grand Prix success for two and a half years.

The lean spell started with a broken con rod in Mexico City, the only occasion that year on which Graham failed to score any F1 points. For the third consecutive season, he finished the championship as runner-up. In Mexico, former team-mate Ginther gave Honda its very first Grand Prix victory. It was regarded as something of a novelty at the time . . .

The 1966 season was a time for change. The F1 regulations were altered to allow three-litre engines. Just as they hadn't been prepared for the last such upheaval, in 1961, BRM weren't ready for the new formula. The complex three-litre H16 required intensive development work (after winning the New Zealand and Australian GPs, Hill flew home early from what had been a successful Tasman Championship in order to speed up its evolution, leaving Stewart to take the title). Plagued by oil feed problems early on, it would not race until the Italian GP in September, so BRM struggled on with its existing 1.5-litre V8s bored out to two litres.

Monaco was a busy place that season, for John Frankenheimer's film crew was on hand to shoot live action sequences for the film *Grand Prix*, in which Hill actually had a speaking part (for around five seconds!). Clark took his customary pole, had his car jam in first gear at the start and finally retired when his suspension collapsed. The mechanical carnage was absolute. Only four cars finished, Hill being the third of them home, an unaccustomed lap in arrears.

After Monte Carlo, Hill headed for Indianapolis where he was scheduled to drive one of John Mecom's George Bignotti-prepared Lolas. The car had originally been intended for Walt Hansgen, but the American veteran had died from injuries received in an accident during the practice weekend for the Le Mans 24 Hours.

After his brief encounter with the Brickyard in 1963, things went rather better this time. Hill qualified on the fifth row, and somehow missed one of Indy's most famous pile-ups, which accounted for one-third of the 33-car field. The red flags were out before most of the grid had reached the first turn.

Once the wreckage had been disentangled and swept away, Jim Clark, looking for a second straight Indy win, moved ahead early on after Mario Andretti blew his engine. Clark lost time with a spectacular spin which sent him scurrying into the pits, and thereafter he duelled long and hard with both Lloyd Ruby and Jackie Stewart – Hill's team-mate. Ruby snuck inside Clark on lap 139 and, with the Lotus due one more stop, the American looked to have the advantage . . . until his engine expired eight laps later.

A third consecutive GP victory in the United States, in
1965, was to be Hill's last World Championship success
for two and a half seasons.

That, reckoned the lap scorers, gave Stewart the lead by almost a full lap from Clark.
Hill was apparently now third. With eight laps to go, Stewart's engine revved its last
and suddenly there was confusion. Hill, who had been receiving pit signals telling him
he was behind Clark, suddenly got the message that he was leading by 18 seconds.

Both the Mecom team and Lotus were signalling to their respective drivers that they
were leading, and the USAC officials agreed with the former. Lotus, they said, had
made a simple lap-scoring error. Lotus, not surprisingly, disagreed.

Hill took the chequered flag and peeled into Victory Lane, where he was fêted by the
regulation beauty queens and supped the glass of milk reserved for the winner. Seconds later, Clark tried to pull into Victory Lane but found that there was already a car-
nival going on. (There were also similar scenes in Hammersmith, west London,
where Bette and friends had watched the event via satellite link at the Odeon cinema.)
The STP Lotus team protested the result, but the following Tuesday USAC declared
– after studying the lap charts and the official race film – that their original decision
would stand.

Hill accepted that it had been a fortuitous victory. To this day, people question who
was right – Team Lotus's lap scorers, or USAC's. Shortly after the victory parade was
over, Clark sidled up to Hill to solicit an honest opinion. Could there have been a mistake? 'No way,' countered the latter. 'I drank the milk.' Lotus subsequently presented
him with an unusual trophy – a milk bottle, complete with baby's teat on top,
mounted on a plinth. There were more serious pecuniary earnings, of course, and the
happy victor bought himself his first private plane, having learned to fly in rare spare
moments during the previous couple of years.

More drama followed in the Belgian GP. The Spa-Francorchamps circuit is notori-
ous for its fickle weather, and the Grand Prix started on a dry track. As the 15 runners
disappeared into the countryside, however, they discovered that the track was soaked.
Several cars left the road at Malmédy, and all three BRMs (American Bob Bondurant
was in a private entry) slithered off at the Masta Kink. Hill's was still drivable, but he
hopped out to attend to Stewart, who was trapped in his overturned car with fuel drip-
ping all around him. Bondurant crawled out of his overturned car, on the other side
of the circuit, to assist, and between them they eventually released him. By that stage,
Hill felt that he'd lost too much time to justify continuing, and he circulated slowly
back to the pits.

Stewart's injuries prevented him from joining Hill at Le Mans, where Brian Muir was
co-opted to share Alan Mann's Ford Mk II, which retired with collapsed front suspension.

The 1966 US GP was to be somewhat ironic. While
BRM struggled to make its H16-engined T83 reliable
(Hill, pictured, retiring with gearbox failure),
Clark won for Lotus using a borrowed version of the
same engine.

The H16 engine had an airing during qualifying for the French GP, but the car's handling still hadn't been sorted to Hill's satisfaction, though there was little doubt that it was more efficient than the stretched two-litre in a straight line. Hill stuck with the old car for the race, and retired with a broken cam. That at least brought a little relief, as he had burnt his backside during the previous day's F2 support race, when his Matra-BRM sprang an oil leak.

A run of points finishes in Britain (third), Holland (second) and Germany (fourth) eventually gave him fifth place in the championship, which Jack Brabham clinched for the third time at the Nürburgring. BRM finally decided to concentrate on the H16 from the Italian Grand Prix onwards, but the season concluded with retirements at Monza, Watkins Glen and in Mexico City. Just to put the boot in, Clark won the American GP running a borrowed BRM H16 in the back of his Lotus . . .

Hill had been with BRM for seven seasons, winning ten races and one World Championship, as well as finishing second in the drivers' table on three occasions. By and large, it had been a happy association, but late in 1966 he received a tempting offer from Lotus, which had entered into partnership with Ford to run a brand new Cosworth-developed V8 the following season.

BRM neophyte: Hill joined the Bourne team in 1960 (inset), though it took a year or two for results to materialise. He finished eighth in the 1961 Dutch GP at Zandvoort (below); one year later he would break his World Championship duck at the same venue.

Overleaf: Hill's first World Championship-winning season included a total of four wins, though in the French GP at Reims he was out of luck, fuel injection problems keeping him out of the points.

Two on the trot: Hill backed up his 1963 Tourist Trophy
success with a repeat performance one year later. His
Ferrari was entered once again by Maranello
Concessionaires, though this time it was a 330P rather
than a GTO.

His luck in Britain never seemed to hold out when
World Championship points were at stake. In 1963, at
Silverstone, he lost second place on the last lap, his car
running out of fuel in the closing seconds and dropping
him to a none the less respectable third place.

The greatest race? Bandini and Surtees tuck Hill into a
Ferrari sandwich during the BRM driver's stupendous
recovery drive at Monaco in 1965.

Back garden GP. Trackside fittings in the 1960s weren't quite in the three-layer Armco mould. Hill heads for fifth place at Spa in 1965.

Before the storm. Stewart, Hill and Gurney confer at Spa in 1966. In the race, Hill retired after losing several laps rescuing BRM team-mate Stewart from his upturned car. The Scot escaped the wreck with a broken wrist.

Ferrari's Mike Parkes, with three litres of Italian grunt at his disposal, wonders where Hill's technically repressed BRM gets its zest in the 1966 French GP. BRM still didn't have a suitable three-litre engine race-ready, and relied on a stretched version of its old 1.5.

'Heads or tails, boss?' The 1967 US GP should have been settled on the toss of a coin. Hill, in conference with Lotus boss Colin Chapman, should have won the event after calling correctly, but reckoned without a broken clutch. He still finished second to team-mate Jim Clark. On home territory, Ford didn't want its drivers' chances compromised by their racing each other too hard . . .

While awaiting the new Cosworth engine, Lotus entered Hill in a variety of different chassis/engine combinations. At Monaco, the wheezy old two-litre BRM was potent enough to propel the Lotus 33 to second place.

Although he never won his home Grand Prix, Graham Hill could do no wrong in Monaco. Ironically, his great rival Jim Clark never achieved the desired success around the streets of the Principality, but had the golden touch on home soil. Here, Hill heads for the fourth of his five Monaco triumphs, hounded by John Surtees's Honda in 1968.

Hill's first points in the Lotus 49-Cosworth came at Mosport Park. Having at one stage had to jump out to give himself a bump-start, he came home fourth, albeit two laps adrift.

Graham Hill, 15 February 1929 – 29 November 1975.

Although Hill was never really a contender in his Brabham days, he enjoyed patches of encouraging form. At Paul Ricard in 1971 he qualified fourth, but fell victim to failing oil pressure. Ronnie Peterson follows.

The master and the pupil. Hill and Tony Brise had
forged a promising alliance, which would surely have
borne fruit had fate not intervened.

As much a part of the fittings at BRM as Jim Clark was at Lotus, Hill nevertheless decided to partner the Scot in 1967, the two drivers being given equal number one status. His contract also included a hectic supplementary schedule of F2 events and saloon car races. In addition, with Clark now setting up home in Paris to escape Britain's Draconian tax requirements and unable to spend much time in the UK, there was a whole development programme with the new Cosworth.

The split with BRM, whose attention was now divided between the Grand Prix team and several contractual obligations outside F1, was entirely amicable. In his first World Championship race for Colin Chapman since 1959, Hill found himself racing a Lotus 43 . . . powered by the BRM H16!

He spun off on his own oil.

For Monaco, he had an older 33 chassis and a rather toothless BRM 2.0. Despite having a gearbox that had been cobbled together out of assorted spares, he held on to take second place behind first-time winner Denny Hulme. There was little joy in Monte Carlo, however, even for Hulme. Lorenzo Bandini, lying second, crashed fatally. The surviving cars picked their way through the burning debris that was strewn across the track for the last 18 laps. Incredibly, no attempt was made to stop the race.

On 4 June, at Zandvoort, Hill sat in pole position for the Dutch GP. He was at the wheel of the brand new Lotus 49, with its Cosworth DFV engine. Team-mate Clark, whose voluntary expatriation meant that he had never sat in the car before, was only eighth, and happy to learn all about the machine's foibles in due course.

Ford had staked a great deal on this new F1 venture, and were not to be disappointed. Hill served immediate notice of the combination's potential by opening up a two-second lead on the first lap. After ten laps, his afternooon was through. He pitted with camshaft trouble, and five laps later Clark had fought his way past Brabham to resume the Lotus-Ford demonstration. Clark, master of the delicate touch, took an effortless victory.

For the team, it was a tremendous fillip. For the opposition, the writing was on the wall. At a stroke, the DFV had rendered other engines obsolete. For Hill, who had done all the development work, it was disappointing, something he would have to get used to over the next few months.

Both drivers qualified on the front row at Spa, but a gearbox problem put paid to Hill while Clark lost time with spark plug breakages, finishing sixth. The cars turned up late for the French GP, held for the only time on Le Mans' Bugatti circuit, after a dispute at a customs post. When they finally arrived Hill took pole, but both cars retired with similar crown wheel and pinion failures.

At Silverstone, Hill suffered the embarrassment of clattering into the wall when he suffered a suspension failure on his way into the pits during practice. A new car was built up overnight, and had to be bedded in during the opening laps of the race. Once settled into his rhythm, Hill moved into the lead, which he held for a total of 29 laps. Then a suspension bolt dislodged itself, a possible consequence of the rush to get the machine ready, and he pitted for repairs. Clark's only threat had been removed. Graham rejoined, only for his engine to expire.

There was another rear suspension failure at the Nürburgring, although Hill was well down the order after being hit at the first corner. In the first-ever Canadian GP at Mosport Park, rather inconveniently inserted between Germany and Italy, Clark led before retiring while Hill finally picked up his first finish since Monaco, and his first points with the Cosworth. In lousy conditions, he had to abandon the cockpit at one point to give himself a push-start, much as he had done at Monaco in 1965. He trailed in fourth, two laps adrift.

In Italy, Hill was leading by almost a lap when his engine blew ten laps from home. Clark, recovering from an early stop to replace a punctured tyre, managed to recoup the lap lost and fought his way into the lead . . . only to stammer, out of fuel, halfway around the last lap.

He crawled home in third place, but Ford wanted to put on an especially good show on their true home soil. The engine had been developed in Europe, but Ford were anxious to fly the corporate flag in the States. Not wanting the two drivers to risk breaking their engines by racing each other, they arranged for Clark and Hill to toss a coin. Hill

won the toss, but lost the race when his clutch packed up. The team duly finished 1-2, but only after Clark had completed the last two laps with his left-rear wheel at a drunken angle following yet another suspension failure.

Clark won again in Mexico, where Hill's barren season ended – after just one lap in the lead – with a halfshaft failure.

There was a four-month gap between the 1968 South African Grand Prix, at Kyalami, and the Spanish race, back on the calendar for the first time since 1954, at Jarama. In the former, Clark and Hill chalked up a comfortable 1-2. In the latter, Lotus entered just one car for Hill, and Colin Chapman wasn't particularly keen to do that.

On 7 April, competing in an inconsequential F2 race at Hockenheim, Clark lost his life when his Lotus 48 inexplicably left the track and hit a tree. He was in his ninth season with the Lotus F1 team; Chapman and his men were utterly devastated.

*Victorious rookie: although he had previously driven at
Indianapolis, 1966 marked the first occasion on which
Hill had actually raced at the Brickyard.*

Bette Hill recalls: 'We were all terribly distraught, and nobody was really in the mood to race in Spain. Colin didn't even go. Graham's win was a real morale-booster.'

If ever a team had needed picking up off the floor it was now, the perfect time for Hill to end his long winning drought. At the wheel of the same 49 chassis that he had placed on pole at Zandvoort almost one year before, he paced himself steadily and profited from the misfortunes of others (notably Pedro Rodriguez and Chris Amon) to move into the championship lead.

At Monaco, he took pole in the new, mildly bewinged 49B (Lotus's first venture into the field of aerodynamics) and led for most of the race, his fourth triumph in the Principality.

These new appendages should logically have made more sense at Spa, where it was announced that Hill had been awarded the OBE, but after a troubled practice he opted to race without them. A broken driveshaft put him out on lap six, though his new team-mate, Jackie Oliver, scored a couple of points in his 49B, having gone far enough to be classified when he suffered a similar failure.

It was the start of a lean spell that eroded Hill's healthy early-season advantage in the championship, and led to a three-way title decider that was rather familiar. At a sodden Zandvoort he crashed out while lying fourth. At Rouen he suffered a broken driveshaft. (It could never happen today dept: while watching the race in France, Hill offered trackside attention to Jo Siffert, who had pulled up nearby with his visor broken. Hill simply offered the Swiss his own, and the latter was able to continue.) The frustration continued at Brands Hatch, where Siffert's privately entered Lotus triumphed after Hill lost a comfortable lead when a universal joint broke.

At the Nürburgring, Hill was up to his old push-start tricks once more. Duelling with Chris Amon for second place behind the expertly driven Matra of Stewart, he spun off, stalled and waited for the crunch. He knew the New Zealander wasn't far behind him. The impact never came. Unseen through the spray in his mirrors, Chris had gone off all on his own earlier that lap. Hill hopped out, got the car rolling and bump-started it back into second place.

The Italian GP at Monza was Hill's 100th, though the event gave little other cause for celebration. He lost a wheel while running in the leading bunch, but at least his championship lead was proving to be more durable than his Lotus, though victory allowed reigning World Champion Denny Hulme to edge into title contention.

Hulme levelled the scores with another win in Canada, but the sinuous St Jovite circuit played havoc with mechanical reliability. Hill finished fourth, four laps down, after suffering an alarming series of engine mounting failures. The G-loads were simply too much for the bolts. When accelerating, the engine would pull away from the bulkhead, causing the chassis to flex alarmingly. The problem was not immediately obvious when the car was at rest in the pits. Eventually it was spotted, and fresh bolts were fitted to allow Hill to score three valuable points.

There was another unforeseen tweak at Watkins Glen, when the steering column started to self-adjust without warning. Under braking, the wheel would slither down towards the dashboard; under acceleration, it would return whence it came, albeit somewhat erratically. Despite the handicap, Hill was the only man other than winner Stewart to go the whole distance. Hulme crashed out early on, so the Lotus driver went to Mexico City with three points in hand over Stewart, six over Hulme.

The title contenders held the top three positions in the early stages of the Mexican GP, until Hulme escaped unscathed from a fiery accident on lap 11, following a suspension breakage. Stewart and Hill then scrapped among themselves for the lead, with sporadic interruptions from Jo Siffert. The latter was delayed by a faulty throttle linkage, Stewart hit fuel feed bothers and Hill was left in the clear. After the devastating loss of Clark back in April, it was fitting that Hill and Team Lotus should emerge as champions.

The press began to speculate that Hill, now approaching 40, might have half an eye on retirement. Graham? He was looking forward to 1969, when he would be joined at Lotus by Jochen Rindt.

It was not to be a good season. There were controversies over the frail-looking wings that were sprouting ever higher on F1 cars, causing problems for Lotus in particular, and Colin Chapman was also a long way down the road to developing a four-wheel drive F1 machine, which ultimately proved to be a blind alley.

Hill started the year brightly enough, with second place to Stewart in South Africa, but he had a sizeable accident in Spain when his rear wing failed on lap eight. Rindt suffered the same fate 11 laps later, although he somehow contrived to have an even bigger accident, amazingly without serious injury to himself. Both cars were junk.

The meeting left Lotus short of chassis, and a couple of 49s were retrieved from Australia to be fettled hurriedly in time for Monaco, where the governing CSI slapped a ban on wings. Rindt was unfit to participate (Richard Attwood substituted), and Hill was reunited with the same chassis that had carried him to his fourth Monaco success one year earlier.

It also gave him a fifth. Chris Amon and Jackie Stewart both led him early on, before succumbing to differential and driveshaft failures respectively. Hill's uncanny knack of preserving his car around this, the most demanding circuit of all, gave him the last of

Final celebration: Hill's fifth Monaco success increased his already considerable popularity. Even in the twilight of his career, he was still fêted by the locals in the Principality.

his 14 Grand Prix victories. Much as he would have liked to win the British GP, it was fitting that his final major F1 success should be in Monte Carlo, where he had made his GP debut some 11 years earlier. Since his first victory there in 1963, his record over seven seasons read: five wins, one second, one third. Truly astonishing. No wonder that, even in the twilight of his career, when he was struggling even to qualify, the Monégasque crowds still peppered him with bouquets.

It also transpired that he had raced at Indianapolis for the last time. In 1968, he had driven a highly fancied Lotus turbine for the STP team which had protested his victory in '66. On that occasion he spun out, and in '69 he didn't get that far, Lotus withdrawing its entries after encountering a series of hub failures in practice.

In Holland, Hill toyed with the four-wheel drive Lotus 63 in qualifying, before opting to stick with the better-sorted 49B. He and returnee Rindt both qualified at the front, but Hill finished seventh after pitting with rear suspension trouble. Handling bothers restricted him to sixth place in France, while Lotus put on an act worthy of Chipperfields at Silverstone. The team's cars arrived late at the circuit, so Hill amused himself by borrowing Ickx's Brabham for a few early practice laps. Lotus eventually delivered one 49B for Rindt, and a brace of the still unproven (John Miles had completed just one racing lap at Clermont-Ferrand) 63s for Hill and Miles.

Hill was not amused, and did a deal to borrow Jo Bonnier's recently acquired 49B, the obliging Swede taking over the 4WD device in exchange. Hill finished seventh, Bonnier (one of a group of four all-wheel drive contenders in a cluster at the back of the grid) blew his engine on lap six.

Thereafter, Hill stuck with the 49B, finishing fourth in Germany despite losing fourth gear. In Italy, he recovered from a poor grid position to join the slipstreaming battle at the front. With five laps to go a driveshaft broke, and he was classified ninth. Stewart won to annex his first world title.

A safe fourth place in the Canadian GP went by the board when the camshaft broke, Hill pulling up behind Miles's 63, which had run in an unusually respectable eighth place before its gearbox seized. Jochen Rindt's win at Watkins Glen, the Austrian's first World Championship victory after several near misses, should have made it a happy day for Team Lotus, but his success was to be overshadowed.

Lying third in the early stages, Hill slipped back to seventh with somewhat unpredictable handling. Eventually, having settled in fifth spot, he spun off on some oil. Unable to restart, he clambered out. Finding nothing amiss, he re-embarked and managed to get going. Still the car felt peculiar. Suspecting a rear puncture, he signalled the pits to prepare a replacement as he passed for the 90th time. On lap 91, the tyre suddenly deflated completely under braking, the car careered into the bank and cartwheeled several times.

Hill, who had been unable to refasten his harness after his spin, was thrown clear. He smashed his knees against the dashboard as he fell, breaking his right knee, dislocating the left and tearing numerous ligaments. It was the only time he ever hurt himself badly in a racing car.

Medical opinion suggested that he wouldn't race for a year. Colin Chapman felt it would be a good time to retire. Graham set himself a target. He wanted to compete in the South African GP next March. It was now 5 October. He was determined that the Mexican GP, in two weeks' time, would be the only one he'd miss.

This was a race that would require even more concentrated effort than the Nürburgring in '62 . . .

It was utterly typical of the man that he should defy all medical forecasts and turn up at Kyalami as something rather more than a spectator. And it was equally predictable that, despite having to be assisted in and out of his Lotus's cockpit (he could still barely walk at this stage), he should finish in the championship points. He was no longer part of Colin Chapman's works operation, but had signed with his good friend Rob Walker to drive a privately entered Lotus 49, similar to that which he had raced during the past three seasons but uprated to the latest 49C specification.

During his unexpectedly rapid recuperation, traditional drugs had completely failed to numb the agony that followed various ligament operations. In the end, the doctors resorted to heroin as a painkiller, happily without causing any hallucinatory side-effects.

While a reluctant tenant at London's University College Hospital, Hill became well acquainted with an exercise bike, which he took to just as soon as he was able, sneaking in extra sessions behind the doctors' backs whenever he could. This abnormally active patient was finally discharged, with walking sticks, just eight weeks before the South African GP. The experts still reckoned on at least six months before he would be able to race a car again . . .

In the event, the gallant returnee qualified on the penultimate row of the 23-car grid, and drove steadily to finish sixth, one lap down, a remarkable result in the circumstances.

Although Rindt (predictably) and local driver Dave Charlton had qualified in the top half of the field at Kyalami with their 49Cs, the writing was on the wall for the ageing chassis. Colin Chapman's revolutionary, wedge-shaped 72 was just around the corner (Rindt would debut the car in the following Spanish GP, though he reverted to the 49C for Monaco, where he won, and Spa).

Hill? He would have to make do with the older design for most of the year, though Jarama proved to be a race of attrition, and he finished fourth. In Monte Carlo, he damaged his chassis in practice and started from the back of the grid after taking over John Miles's non-qualified works car. Given a fresh coat of 'Walker Racing Blue' overnight, it brought him home in fifth place. He was the only driver to have scored points in the opening three races, and at that stage he lay fifth in the World Championship.

Thereafter, Hill's fortunes slipped a little. The private Lotus was a regular fixture on the back row of the grid for the next few races, though he bagged his final point of the year at Brands Hatch, where he did well to finish sixth without a clutch. An engine failure rounded off a miserable German GP weekend and the team skipped Austria to await delivery of a 72, with which Rindt had by now won four Grands Prix on the trot, in Holland, France, Britain and Germany.

The car was ready for Monza, but the team withdrew as a mark of respect for Jochen Rindt, after the World Championship leader was mortally injured during qualifying. The Austrian's five victories to that point would be enough to make him the sport's first posthumous World Champion.

Hill finally raced a 72 for the first time in Canada, qualifying last and dropping out with gearbox trouble. There was a dramatic upturn in practice form for the final two races of the year, but clutch failure at Watkins Glen (where he ran seventh in the early stages) and a blown engine in Mexico City left him 13th in the championship thanks to his early-season consistency.

Bette remembers 1970 fondly, in some respects. 'It wasn't terribly successful in terms of results, bearing in mind what Graham had become used to, but Rob and Betty Walker were such wonderful people to be with that it was still an enjoyable stage of his career.'

Most of the time, that was. In addition to Rindt's fatal accident, Piers Courage had been killed during the Dutch GP and Bruce McLaren had perished while testing one of his eponymous CanAm cars at Goodwood. It had been one of motor racing's more brutal seasons.

The face of the sport was changing in other ways too; Jack Brabham, soon to be Sir Jack, was retiring. Before the start of his final season, he'd sold control of the team which carried his name to erstwhile partner Ron Tauranac, and it was here that Hill found himself at the beginning of 1971.

His association with Brabham lasted for two seasons, but brought little real joy in terms of F1 results. As senior member of the 1971 line-up, Hill was entrusted, from the second race onwards, with the one-off BT34 'lobster claw' chassis, while team-mate Tim Schenken made do with the previous season's BT33.

After a ninth-place finish with a BT33 in South Africa, where he was delayed by a startline collision, the BT34's first GP, in Spain, netted an early retirement with steering damage. This was a disappointment, for one month earlier Hill had challenged Jackie Stewart for second place in the Race of Champions at Brands Hatch, before buzzing his engine with a missed gearshift. As consolation, he went away with fastest lap in his pocket.

After Spain, optimism was further kindled by outright victory in the International Trophy at Silverstone, where Hill profited from Jackie Stewart's high-speed exit into the barriers at Copse. It was a popular success, and proved significant in that it was to be his last in an F1 car.

In Monte Carlo, a couple of weeks later, the five-times winner qualified ninth, but he was unable to maintain his remarkable run of scoring points in every Monaco GP since his first championship-winning season in 1962 (when he was classified sixth, despite suffering a late-race engine failure while leading). On the second lap he tapped the barriers on the inside at Tabac, spearing back across the track to smite the guard rail opposite and retire minus a couple of wheels and sundry other ancillaries.

As the year wore on, Hill increasingly found himself outpaced by his more youthful team-mate, who had struck up a better rapport with Tauranac. There were occasional highlights, however. At Paul Ricard, where the French GP was held for the first time, he qualified fourth and stayed with the leading group until spinning on his own oil.

At Silverstone, Hill was again well down after a series of engine failures in qualifying. He retired almost as the race started, being struck from behind by Jackie Oliver's McLaren. After coming home ninth at the Nürburgring, he finally scored his only points of the season in Austria, finishing fifth. He would eventually be classified 21st in the championship, after a largely barren season. Nevertheless, there had been some light relief earlier on, between the non-championship British F1 races during which the BT34 had flattered to deceive.

Hill also had a busy F2 programme to fit in, mainly driving a Brabham BT36 for Rondel Racing, which served as a vehicle for Ron Dennis's formative years in racing management. At Hockenheim, he took the BT36 to a heat win in, appropriately, the Jim Clark Memorial Trophy, eventually taking second on aggregate to Francois Cevert. One week later he won at Thruxton, beating eventual European F2 Champion Ronnie Peterson.

Brabham changed hands more radically in 1972, when Tauranac sold out to Bernie Ecclestone. Initially, it appeared there was no place for Hill, as rising Argentine star Carlos Reutemann had graduated from F2 to partner Schenken. When Tauranac left, however, the latter followed . . . and Graham retained his place, although the BT34 was conferred on Reutemann. Schenken's old BT33, mildly updated, was offered to Hill, until such time as the BT37, penned by Tauranac's successor Ralph Bellamy, was ready.

In fact Hill was entrusted with the BT37 for its debut, in the International Trophy at Silverstone. He finished a workmanlike seventh.

Prior to that, he'd taken his first point of the season, finishing sixth with the ageing BT33 in South Africa. As in 1971, championship points were scarce, though there were a couple more top-six finishes this time. He was sixth again with the BT37 in Germany and fifth in Italy, which put him joint 12th in the final standings. He had been outpaced all season, however, by both Reutemann and Wilson Fittipaldi, who had joined the team in Spain, concentrating mainly on the by then redundant BT34 thereafter.

As far as F1 was concerned, Hill's mind was now tracking a different course. Clearly, he was in the twilight of his Grand Prix career, and with no offers forthcoming from elsewhere he turned his thoughts to setting up his own F1 team. (He was already running his own F2 Brabham.)

But 1972 wasn't all gloom and despondency. In June, he scored two victories. One was in the Monza Lottery F2 race, at the wheel of the aforementioned Brabham BT38. The other was in a works-entered Matra–Simca MS670.

In 1972, Graham Hill became the first driver ever to have won the World Championship, Indianapolis 500 *and* the Le Mans 24 Hours. He was no stranger to the Sarthe classic, of course. The invitation to join the crack Matra team, whose preparations included near-permanent residence at Paul Ricard in order to carry out extensive endurance testing, was all the same a pleasant surprise. This was Hill's tenth participation in the event, but his first since 1966.

He was signed to accompany Frenchman Henri Pescarolo, who duly qualified the car second. Matra, who eschewed any other involvement in the World Championship of Makes, as it was then called, was confident that its V12 would run flat out for the duration.

This optimism wasn't exactly buoyed by the sight of Jean-Pierre Beltoise's sister car erupting in flames as early as lap two, but the other Matras proved to be more reliable. The Pescarolo/Hill combo exchanged the lead with team-mates François Cevert and Howden Ganley in the first part of the race, but the Franco-Antipodean pair eventually lost several laps with a variety of irritating problems, including a savaging from a Chevrolet Corvette on the Mulsanne Straight.

Making metronomic progress, Hill and Pescarolo eventually won the race by ten clear laps from Cevert and Ganley. The occasion was marred, however, by the death of Jo Bonnier, whose Lola left the track and flew into some trees early on the Sunday morning. Bonnier was one of Hill's oldest friends in racing, his BRM team-mate in 1960 and co-driver of the Ferrari P3 with which he had recorded his previous best result at Le Mans, second place in 1964. Momentous as it had been, it was something of a sorrowful victory.

Although his F1 star was in the descendant by 1972,
Hill still had other diversions to amuse him. At Le
Mans, he and Henri Pescarolo gave Matra the victory
it craved on home soil. Hill became the first, and only,
World Champion to add victories in the Indianapolis
500 and Le Mans 24 Hours to his CV.

Hill's 'Triple Crown' looks unlikely ever to be equalled if the sport continues to follow its present course. The modern-day Grand Prix driver is more often than not prevented, contractually, from doing anything other than F1, in an age when there are 16 Grand Prix weekends and most of the gaps in between are dedicated to constant testing.

During 1972, the fledgling F2 entrant opened negotiations with John Wilson from Embassy, in an effort to secure finance for his new F1 project. A deal was put together and thus it was that the Embassy Hill Grand Prix team took shape in workshops at Feltham, not far from Heathrow Airport.

Shadow was a new F1 manufacturer, and it agreed to supply a chassis to Hill in addition to running its own UOP-supported cars for Jackie Oliver and George Follmer. The latter weren't ready for the opening races in South America, and first appeared at Kyalami in March. Hill's season commenced with the Race of Champions at Brands Hatch (in a Brabham BT37, which he retired after a collision), and he didn't make his seasonal F1 debut in his new Shadow until Spain, where he was plagued by brake trouble. After qualifying last, he retired.

Belgium brought little improvement, a plug lead coming adrift and forcing him to trundle around at the back. He was eventually classified ninth, five laps down, which was to be his best result of the year, albeit not necessarily his best performance . . .

In short, the season was a catalogue of woes. Hill retired from six of the 12 races he contested. In qualifying, he only scaled the less than dizzy heights of the lower midfield on a couple of occasions.

His only other outing was in the Spa 1000 Kilometres sports car race, at Matra's behest. In keeping with the pattern of the season, engine failure consigned him to retirement.

Volume racing car constructor Lola was commissioned to produce an F1 car for the Hill team's exclusive use in 1974, when Graham planned to run a brace of cars for himself and Formula 5000 front-runner Guy Edwards. Lola chief Eric Broadley came up with the T370, the Huntingdon firm's first direct involvement with F1 since the early 1960s.

The cars proved to be generally reliable, though the chassis was never quicker than when Rolf Stommelen was drafted in to replace Edwards in mid-season, the latter having broken a wrist while racing in Formula 5000. It was Hill, however, who scored the team's first World Championship point, poignantly the last of his own career, in the Swedish GP at Anderstorp. He finished 11 of the 15 races, six of them in the top ten.

Stommelen's performances guaranteed him a place alongside Hill for 1975, when the team retained its T370s for the opening races. Hill finished 10th and 12th respectively in Argentina and Brazil, just leading home his team-mate on each occasion.

In South Africa, extensive chassis reworking by Andy Smallman led to Stommelen's machine being entered as a T371. The German finished an encouraging seventh in a car which only turned a wheel for the first time that weekend, but Hill scratched after writing off the team's older chassis in the opening moments of the first practice session, an oil slick dropped by Ronnie Peterson's Lotus sending him flying off the circuit.

The cars were rechristened again by the time the Spanish GP came around, this time rolling out of the truck as Hill GH1s. This was the first official Grand Prix appearance of a Hill chassis, although Hill himself had raced one under the same appellation in Silverstone's non-championship International Trophy.

The International Trophy would not only mark Graham's final F1 victory (with Brabham in 1971). In 1975, it also gave him his final F1 race. He finished a lowly 11th, harried all the way to the flag by Lella Lombardi's March.

In Spain, Hill stood down to make way for French journeyman François Migault. Stommelen again proved to be the team's prize asset, however, picking his way through the debris of a startline collision which eliminated both Ferraris to run fourth in the early stages. He moved up to lead from the 17th lap until his rear wing collapsed on the 26th. The Hill smashed into and vaulted over the barriers, landing amid a small cluster of onlookers standing outside the official spectator enclosures. There were four fatalities among the bystanders, while the unfortunate German – later to lose his life in a sports car race at Riverside in 1983 – was stretchered off with both legs broken and assorted lesser injuries. The race was abandoned after 29 laps; ironically, reigning World Champion Emerson Fittipaldi had refused to take part, completing just a slow token practice lap in protest at safety standards at the Montjuich Park circuit.

The team naturally entered just one car for Monaco, where Hill couldn't resist one last crack. At this stage, there had still been no formal statement about his future driving plans, but a few people suspected that an official retirement announcement was around the corner.

In Monte Carlo, Hill swapped between the GH1 and an old Lola, but only wound up 21st fastest. At the time, the circuit was licensed only for 18 starters. A couple of well-meaning associates set about trying to persuade Prince Rainier to pull a few strings to get Hill onto a Monaco grid for one last time. Unsurprisingly, they failed . . .

Hill stepped down again in Belgium, where he recruited the promising young Briton Tony Brise, who had made his Grand Prix debut in the ill-fated Spanish race for Williams one month earlier. A second car was entered for Migault, but it was the Englishman who commanded most of the team proprietor's attention. Since embarking upon the F1 scheme in 1973 he'd found it hard to give either team management or driving the level of commitment that both roles needed. In Brise, he'd found an ideal driver around whom to build the Embassy Hill team.

Brise qualified a promising eighth but his race was cut short when his DFV dropped a piston. Hill liked what he'd seen, however, and during that weekend at Zolder he made his mind up. He would retire from active race driving, though he wasn't quite ready to share his decision with the world as yet. Ever the showman, he saved his announcement for the eve of his home Grand Prix at Silverstone, where, to a tumultuous ovation, he completed a farewell lap before the start of the race.

In 18 seasons of Formula 1 racing, Graham Hill had started 176 Grands Prix, winning 14 of them, collecting 289 points and two World Championship titles.

Before announcing his retirement, there were still three Grands Prix to oversee, Brise scoring a first championship point in the next race at Anderstorp, where Vern Schuppan had his only drive for the team. The Australian was replaced in Holland by countryman Alan Jones, who partnered Brise until Stommelen was fit to return to the cockpit in Austria.

Brise continued to show promise, finishing seventh in both Holland and France and generally qualifying well, his best practice effort earning a third-row start at Monza. By general consensus, he was the F1 discovery of the season.

Jones bagged a brace of points in Germany, his last appearance before Stommelen's return, and the Hill team finished 11th in the Constructors' Cup in its first season as an F1 manufacturer.

By the season's end, Embassy had agreed to continue sponsoring the team into 1976, and British motor sport was looking forward to what 23-year-old Brise might achieve under Hill's guidance, with the new Andy Smallman-designed GH2.

On 29 November, the nucleus of the Hill team, Graham, Tony Brise, Smallman, team manager Ray Brimble and mechanics Terry Richards and Tony Alcock, were all returning together in Hill's six-seater Piper Aztec twin from what proved to be the GH2's final test session at Paul Ricard.

On that foggy Saturday night, Britain lost one of its most famous, and undoubtedly finest, sporting ambassadors, and the bright hopes of a most promising new racing team were cruelly extinguished.

GRAHAM HILL
CAREER RECORD · 1956–1975
BY STEVE SMALL

1956

	Race	Circuit	Date	Entrant	Car	Comment
1	Up to 1200 cc Sports Car Race	Brands Hatch	29/04/56	Team Lotus	Lotus XI-Climax	
2	Up to 1500 cc Sports Car Race	Brands Hatch	29/04/56	Team Lotus	Lotus XI-Climax	*broke 1500 cc lap record*
3	Farningham Trophy	Brands Hatch	21/05/56	Equipe Endeavour	Cooper-Climax	
6	Wrotham Cup	Brands Hatch	21/05/56	Equipe Endeavour	Cooper-Climax	*handicap race*
3	Anerley Trophy	Crystal Palace	22/05/56	Tommy Sopwith	Lotus XI-Climax	
3	Norbury Trophy	Crystal Palace	22/05/56	Tommy Sopwith	Lotus XI-Climax	
1	Up to 1200 cc Production Race	Mallory Park	08/06/56	J.J. Richards	Lotus XI-Ford	
1	*Autosport* Championship Race	Aintree	23/06/56	J.J. Richards	Lotus XI-Ford	
7	Sports/Formula 2 Race	Silverstone	14/07/56	J.J. Richards	Lotus XI-Ford	
dsq	*Autosport* Trophy Race	Brands Hatch	06/08/56	J.J. Richards	Lotus XI-Ford	
3	Class 1B Hillclimb	Prescott	08/09/56	J.J. Richards	Lotus XI-Ford	
ret	*Autosport* 3-Hour Race	Oulton Park	22/09/56	J.J. Richards	Lotus XI-Ford	*engine*
ret	Sports Car Race	Snetterton	07/10/56	Tommy Sopwith	Lotus XI-Ford	*bent steering arm*
5	Sports/Formula 2 Race	Brands Hatch	14/10/56	J.J. Richards	Lotus XI-Ford	
2	Up to 1200 cc Sports Car Race	Brands Hatch	14/10/56	J.J. Richards	Lotus XI-Ford	

1957

	Race	Circuit	Date	Entrant	Car	Comment
1	Up to 1100 cc Sports Car Race	Brands Hatch	31/03/57	Dr E. Manton	Lotus XI-Climax	
1	Up to 1200 cc Sports Car Race	Oulton Park	06/04/57	Dr E. Manton	Lotus XI-Climax	
5	Lavant Cup	Goodwood	22/04/57	T.C. Atkins	Connaught F2	
4	Chichester Cup	Goodwood	22/04/57	Dr E. Manton	Lotus XI-Climax	*(1st 1100 cc class)*
9	Sussex Trophy	Goodwood	22/04/57	T.C. Atkins	Aston Martin DB3S	
1	Up to 1100 cc Sports Car Race	Brands Hatch	19/05/57	Dr E. Manton	Lotus XI-Climax	
3	Unlimited Sports Car Race	Brands Hatch	19/05/57	T.C. Atkins	Aston Martin DB3S	
4	Up to 1100 cc Sports Car Race	Brands Hatch	09/06/57	Dr E. Manton	Lotus XI-Climax	
4	Anerley Trophy	Crystal Palace	10/06/57	Dr E. Manton	Lotus XI-Climax	
ret	Up to 1100 cc Sports Car Race	Snetterton	28/07/57	Dr E. Manton	Lotus XI-Climax	
5	Vanwall Formula Libre Trophy	Snetterton	28/07/57	Dr E. Manton	Lotus XI-Climax	
1	Up to 1100 cc Sports Car Race	Brands Hatch	05/08/57	Dr E. Manton	Lotus XI-Climax	
2	Up to 1500 cc Sports Car Race	Brands Hatch	05/08/57	John Willment	Willment 1500 cc	
2	Kingsdown Trophy	Brands Hatch	05/08/57	John Ogier	Tojeiro-Jaguar	
2	Up to 1250 cc Sports Car Race	Goodwood	31/08/57	Dr E. Manton	Lotus XI-Climax	
ret	Over 1500 cc Sports Car Race	Silverstone	14/09/57	John Ogier	Tojeiro-Jaguar	*suspension*
8	International Trophy – Qual. Heat 2	Silverstone	14/09/57	John Willment	Cooper-Climax F2	*4th F2 class*
13	International Trophy – Final	Silverstone	14/09/57	John Willment	Cooper-Climax F2	*5th F2 class*
5	Woodcote Cup	Goodwood	28/09/57	Team Lotus	Lotus 12-Climax F2	
11	International Gold Cup	Oulton Park	05/10/57	Team Lotus	Lotus 12-Climax F2	*Fastest lap*
1	Christmas Trophy	Brands Hatch	26/12/57	Dr E. Manton	Lotus XI-Climax	

1958

2	Lavant Cup (F2)	Goodwood	07/04/58	Team Lotus	Lotus 12-Climax F2	
ret	Glover Trophy (F1/F2)	Goodwood	07/04/58	Team Lotus	Lotus 12-Climax F2	
ret	Sussex Trophy	Goodwood	07/04/58	Team Lotus	Lotus 15-Climax	
6*	British Empire Trophy	Oulton Park	12/04/58	Team Lotus	Lotus 15-Climax	gear trouble
ret	Over 1100 cc Sports Car Race	Aintree	19/04/58	Team Lotus	Lotus 15-Climax	*Fastest lap/heat 2
4*	Aintree 200	Aintree	19/04/58	Team Lotus	Lotus 16-Climax F2	gearbox
1	Sports Car Race	Silverstone	03/05/58	Team Lotus	Lotus 15-Climax	*(F2 class)
8	*Daily Express* International Trophy	Silverstone	03/05/58	Team Lotus	Lotus 12-Climax	
3	Touring Car Race	Silverstone	03/05/58	Speedwell Racing	Austin A35	
ret	**MONACO GP**	Monte Carlo	18/05/58	Team Lotus	Lotus 12-Climax	lost wheel
ret	**DUTCH GP**	Zandvoort	25/05/58	Team Lotus	Lotus 12-Climax	engine
ret	Coupe de Vitesse	Reims	06/06/58	Team Lotus	Lotus 16-Climax F2	
2	Rouen GP	Rouen	08/06/58	Team Lotus	Lotus 15-Climax	
ret	**BELGIAN GP**	Spa	16/06/58	Team Lotus	Lotus 12-Climax	engine
ret	Le Mans 24 Hours	Le Mans	21-22/06/58	Team Lotus	Lotus 15-Climax 2 litre	c/d Allison/overheating
ret	**FRENCH GP**	Reims	06/07/58	Team Lotus	Lotus 16-Climax	engine
ret	**BRITISH GP**	Silverstone	19/07/58	Team Lotus	Lotus 16-Climax	oil pressure
ret	*Daily Express* Sports Car Race	Silverstone	19/07/58	Team Lotus	Lotus 15-Climax	thrown rod
ret	Touring Car Race	Silverstone	19/07/58	Speedwell Racing	Austin A35	overheating
ret	**GERMAN GP**	Nürburgring	03/08/58	Team Lotus	Lotus 16-Climax	oil pipe
ret	**PORTUGUESE GP**	Oporto	28/08/58	Team Lotus	Lotus 16-Climax	spun off
ret	Kentish Trophy	Brands Hatch	30/08/58	Team Lotus	Lotus 16-Climax	ret heat 2–gearbox
2	Farningham Trophy	Brands Hatch	30/08/58	Team Lotus	Lotus 15-Climax	
6	**ITALIAN GP**	Monza	07/09/58	Team Lotus	Lotus 16-Climax	
ret	Tourist Trophy	Goodwood	13/09/58	Team Lotus	Lotus 15-Climax	c/d Allison/dropped valve
ret	Sports Car Race	Oulton Park	20/09/58	Team Lotus	Lotus 15-Climax	ignition
1*	Over 1100 cc Sports Car Race	Snetterton	11/10/58	Team Lotus	Lotus 15-Climax	*over 1100 cc class
16	**MOROCCAN GP**	Casablanca	19/10/58	Team Lotus	Lotus 16-Climax	
1	Sports Car Race	Brands Hatch	26/12/58	Team Lotus	Lotus Seven	beat Lotus XIs
1	Formula Libre	Brands Hatch	26/12/58	Team Lotus	Lotus 16-Climax F2	

1959

ret	International 100	Goodwood	30/03/59	Team Lotus	Lotus 16-Climax F1	brakes
4	Lavant Cup	Goodwood	30/03/59	Team Lotus	Lotus 16-Climax F2	
ret	British Empire Trophy	Oulton Park	11/04/59	Team Lotus	Lotus 16-Climax F2	engine vibration
4	Unlimited Sports Car Race	Oulton Park	11/04/59	Team Lotus	Lotus 17-2 litre	
2	Over 1500 cc Sports Car Race	Aintree	18/04/59	Team Lotus	Lotus 17-2 litre	
5	Aintree 200	Aintree	18/04/59	Team Lotus	Lotus 16-Climax F1	
ret	Syracuse GP	Syracuse	25/04/59	Team Lotus	Lotus 16-Climax F2	broken rear hub
ret	1100-3000 cc Sports Car Race	Silverstone	02/05/59	Team Lotus	Lotus 17-2 litre	c. w. pinion
ret	*Daily Express* International Trophy	Silverstone	02/05/59	Team Lotus	Lotus 16-Climax F1	brake pipe
ret	**MONACO GP**	Monte Carlo	10/05/59	Team Lotus	Lotus 16-Climax F1	fire
3	Over 1500 cc Sports Car Race	Crystal Palace	18/05/59	Team Lotus	Lotus 17-2 litre	
ret	Formula 2 Race	Mallory Park	25/05/59	Team Lotus	Lotus 16-Climax F2	engine
3	Up to 1100 cc Sports Car Race	Mallory Park	25/05/59	Team Lotus	Lotus XI-Climax	
1	Over 1100 cc Sports Car Race	Mallory Park	25/05/59	Team Lotus	Lotus 15-Climax	
7	**DUTCH GP**	Zandvoort	31/05/59	Team Lotus	Lotus 16-Climax F1	
ret	Le Mans 24 Hours	Le Mans	20-21/06/59	Team Lotus	Lotus 17-Climax	c/d Jolly
ret	Coupe de Vitesse	Reims	04/07/59	Team Lotus	Lotus 16-Climax F2	engine
ret	**FRENCH GP**	Reims	05/07/59	Team Lotus	Lotus 16-Climax F1	radiator
ret	Sports Car Race	Rouen	12/07/59	Team Lotus	Lotus 750 cc	steering
7	Rouen GP	Rouen	12/07/59	Team Lotus	Lotus 16-Climax F2	
9	**BRITISH GP**	Aintree	18/07/59	Team Lotus	Lotus 16-Climax F1	
1	Sports Car Race	Aintree	18/07/59	Team Lotus	Lotus 17-2 litre	
6	Auvergne Trophy	Clermont-Ferrand	26/07/59	Team Lotus	Lotus 16-Climax F2	
ret	**GERMAN GP**	Avus	02/08/59	Team Lotus	Lotus 16-Climax F1	gearbox – heat 1
3	Wrotham Trophy	Brands Hatch	03/08/59	Team Lotus	Lotus XI-Climax	
1	Kingsdown Trophy	Brands Hatch	03/08/59	Team Lotus	Lotus 17-Climax	
ret	John Davy Trophy	Brands Hatch	03/08/59	Team Lotus	Lotus 16-Climax F2	burst oil-cooler
ret	**PORTUGUESE GP**	Monsanto	23/08/59	Team Lotus	Lotus 16-Climax F1	spun off on oil
2	Kentish 100 – Heat 1	Brands Hatch	29/08/59	Team Lotus	Lotus 16-Climax F2	
2	Kentish 100 – Heat 2	Brands Hatch	29/08/59	Team Lotus	Lotus 16-Climax F2	2nd overall
3	Rochester Trophy	Brands Hatch	29/08/59	Team Lotus	Lotus 17-Climax	
1	Farningham Trophy	Brands Hatch	29/08/59	Team Lotus	Lotus 17-2.5 litre	
ret	Tourist Trophy	Goodwood	05/09/59	Team Lotus	Lotus 17-2 litre	c/d Stacey/accident
ret	**ITALIAN GP**	Monza	13/09/59	Team Lotus	Lotus 16-Climax F1	transmission
5	Gold Cup	Oulton Park	26/09/59	Team Lotus	Lotus 16-Climax F1	
1	Up to 1100 cc Sports Car Race	Brands Hatch	04/10/59	Team Lotus	Lotus XI-Climax	
1	Touring Car Race	Brands Hatch	04/10/59	Speedwell Racing	Austin A35	
ret	Silver City Trophy	Snetterton	10/10/59	Team Lotus	Lotus 16-Climax F1	broken driveshaft

1960

3	Buenos Aires 1000 Km	Buenos Aires	31/01/60	Porsche System Engineering	Porsche RSK	c/d Bonnier (1st in class)
ret	**ARGENTINE GP**	Buenos Aires	07/02/60	BRM/Owen Racing Organisation	BRM P25	broken valve spring
ret	Sebring 12 Hours	Sebring	26/03/60	Porsche System Engineering	Porsche RSK	c/d Bonnier/thrown rod
5	International 100	Goodwood	18/04/60	BRM/Owen Racing Organisation	BRM P48	
3	Aintree 200	Aintree	30/04/60	Porsche System Engineering	Porsche F2	
5	Targa Florio	Madonie Circuit	08/05/60	Porsche System Engineering	Porsche RSK	c/d Barth
3	*Daily Express* International Trophy	Silverstone	14/05/60	BRM/Owen Racing Organisation	BRM P48	
ret	Nürburgring 1000 Km	Nürburgring	22/05/60	Porsche System Engineering	Porsche RSK	c/d Barth/crashed
ret	**MONACO GP**	Monte Carlo	29/05/60	BRM/Owen Racing Organisation	BRM P48	crashed
3	**DUTCH GP**	Zandvoort	05/06/60	BRM/Owen Racing Organisation	BRM P48	
2*	Rouen GP	Rouen	07/06/60	Speedwell Racing	Speedwell Sprite	*up to 1100 cc class
ret	**BELGIAN GP**	Spa	19/06/60	BRM/Owen Racing Organisation	BRM P48	blown engine
ret	Le Mans 24 Hours	Le Mans	25-26/06/60	Porsche System Engineering	Porsche RSK	c/d Bonnier/engine
ret	**FRENCH GP**	Reims	03/07/60	BRM/Owen Racing Organisation	BRM P48	shunted on grid
ret	**BRITISH GP**	Silverstone	16/07/60	BRM/Owen Racing Organisation	BRM P48	spun off/Fastest lap
4	Solitude GP	Solitude	24/07/60	Porsche System Engineering	Porsche F2	
4	German GP	Nürburgring	31/07/60	Porsche System Engineering	Porsche F2	
2	Silver City Trophy	Brands Hatch	01/08/60	BRM/Owen Racing Organisation	BRM P48	
ret	**PORTUGUESE GP**	Oporto	14/08/60	BRM/Owen Racing Organisation	BRM P48	gearbox
4	Tourist Trophy	Goodwood	20/08/60	Porsche System Engineering	Porsche Carrera	c/d Abarth (1st in class)
4	Kentish 100	Brands Hatch	27/08/60	Porsche System Engineering	Porsche F2	
ret	Lombank Trophy	Snetterton	17/09/60	BRM/Owen Racing Organisation	BRM P48	engine
3	Gold Cup	Oulton Park	24/09/60	BRM/Owen Racing Organisation	BRM P48	
7	1000 Km de Paris	Montlhéry	23/10/60	Porsche System Engineering	Porsche Carrera	c/d von Hanstein
ret	**US GP**	Riverside	20/11/60	BRM/Owen Racing Organisation	BRM P48	gearbox

1961

3	New Zealand GP	Ardmore	07/01/61	Owen Racing Organisation	BRM P48	
ret	International 100	Warwick Farm	05/02/61	Owen Racing Organisation	BRM P48	leaking fuel tank
1	Formula Libre – Heat 1	Ballarat	12/02/61	Owen Racing Organisation	BRM P48	
2	Formula Libre – Final	Ballarat	12/02/61	Owen Racing Organisation	BRM P48	
ret	Sebring 12 Hours	Sebring	25/03/61	Camoradi International	Maserati T61	c/d Moss/exhaust manifold
3	Lavant Cup	Goodwood	03/04/61	Owen Racing Organisation	BRM P48-Climax	
2	St Mary's Trophy	Goodwood	03/04/61	Equipe Endeavour	Jaguar 3.8	
2	Glover Trophy	Goodwood	03/04/61	Owen Racing Organisation	BRM P48/57-Climax	
1	GT Race	Oulton Park	15/04/61	Equipe Endeavour	Jaguar E-type	
2	Sports Car Race	Oulton Park	15/04/61	UDT-Laystall Racing	Lotus 19-Climax	
3	Aintree 200	Aintree	22/04/61	Owen Racing Organisation	BRM P48/57-Climax	
nc	Syracuse GP	Syracuse	25/04/61	Owen Racing Organisation	BRM P48/57-Climax	engine trouble
1	Production Car Race	Silverstone	06/05/61	Equipe Endeavour	Jaguar 3.8	
ret	*Daily Express* International Trophy	Silverstone	06/05/61	Owen Racing Organisation	BRM P48/57-Climax	
ret	**MONACO GP**	Monte Carlo	14/05/61	Owen Racing Organisation	BRM P48/57-Climax	fuel pump
8	**DUTCH GP**	Zandvoort	22/05/61	Owen Racing Organisation	BRM P48/57-Climax	
ret	Nürburgring 1000 Km	Nürburgring	28/05/61	Porsche S. E./Camoradi Racing	Porsche RSK	c/d Moss/engine
8	Nürburgring 1000 Km	Nürburgring	28/05/61	Porsche System Engineering	Porsche Carrera Prototype	c/d Moss/Linge/Greger
13	Silver City Trophy	Brands Hatch	03/06/61	Owen Racing Organisation	BRM P48/57-Climax	
3	Peco Trophy GT Race	Brands Hatch	03/06/61	Equipe Endeavour	Jaguar E-type	
ret	Le Mans 24 Hours	Le Mans	09-10/06/61	NART	Ferrari 250GT	c/d Moss/water leak
ret	**BELGIAN GP**	Spa	18/06/61	Owen Racing Organisation	BRM P48/57-Climax	oil leak
ret	Targa Florio	Madonie Circuit	30/06/61	Camoradi International	Porsche RSK	c/d Moss/broken differential
6	**FRENCH GP**	Reims	02/07/61	Owen Racing Organisation	BRM P48/57-Climax	
3	British Empire Trophy	Silverstone	08/07/61	Owen Racing Organisation	BRM P48/57-2.5 litre	
2	Touring Car Race	Silverstone	08/07/61	Equipe Endeavour	Jaguar 3.8	
ret	GT Race	Silverstone	08/07/61	Equipe Endeavour	Jaguar E-type	
ret	**BRITISH GP**	Aintree	15/07/61	Owen Racing Organisation	BRM P48/57-Climax	valve spring
ret	**GERMAN GP**	Nürburgring	06/08/61	Owen Racing Organisation	BRM P48/57-Climax	accident
ret	Peco Trophy	Brands Hatch	07/08/61	Equipe Endeavour	Jaguar E-type	puncture
3	Guards Trophy	Brands Hatch	07/08/61	Owen Racing Organisation	BRM P48/57-2.5 litre	
6*	Tourist Trophy	Goodwood	19/08/61	Porsche System Engineering	Porsche Abarth	*1st in class
7	Modena GP	Modena	03/09/61	Owen Racing Organisation	BRM P48/57-Climax	
ret	**ITALIAN GP**	Monza	10/09/61	Owen Racing Organisation	BRM P48/57-Climax	engine
ret	Gold Cup	Oulton Park	23/09/61	Owen Racing Organisation	BRM P48/57-Climax	
2	Production Car Race	Oulton Park	23/09/61	Equipe Endeavour	Jaguar E-type	
5	**US GP**	Watkins Glen	08/10/61	Owen Racing Organisation	BRM P48/57-Climax	
12	Paris 1000 Km	Montlhéry	15/10/61	Scuderia Serenissima	Ferrari 250GT	c/d Bonnier
5	Nassau Trophy	Nassau	10/12/61	Scuderia Serenissima	Ferrari Testa Rossa	
1	Christmas Trophy	Brands Hatch	26/12/61	Scuderia Serenissima	Ferrari Testa Rossa	

1962

dns	Sebring 12 Hours	Sebring	24/03/62	Scuderia Serenissima	Ferrari 2.9 litre	injured back
1	Brussels GP – Heat 1	Heysel	01/04/62	Owen Racing Organisation	BRM P57-V8	
dsq	Brussels GP – Heat 2	Heysel	01/04/62	Owen Racing Organisation	BRM P57-V8	push-start
2	GT Race	Oulton Park	07/04/62	John Coombs	Jaguar E-type	
3	Touring Car Race	Snetterton	14/04/62	John Coombs	Jaguar Mk II 3.8	
2	Lombank Trophy	Snetterton	14/04/62	Owen Racing Organisation	BRM P57-V8	
1	Glover Trophy	Goodwood	23/04/62	Owen Racing Organisation	BRM P57-V8	
1	St Mary's Trophy	Goodwood	23/04/62	John Coombs	Jaguar Mk II 3.8	
1	Saloon Car Race	Aintree	28/04/62	John Coombs	Jaguar Mk II 3.8	
ret	Aintree '200'	Aintree	28/04/62	Owen Racing Organisation	BRM P57-V8	
1	Daily Express International Trophy	Silverstone	12/05/62	Owen Racing Organisation	BRM P57-V8	
3	GT Race	Silverstone	12/05/62	John Coombs	Jaguar E-type	
1	Touring Car Race	Silverstone	12/05/62	John Coombs	Jaguar Mk II 3.8	
1	**DUTCH GP**	Zandvoort	20/05/62	Owen Racing Organisation	BRM P57-V8	
3	Nürburgring 1000 Km	Nürburgring	27/05/62	Porsche System Engineering	Porsche F8	c/d Herrmann (1st in class)
6/ret	**MONACO GP**	Monte Carlo	03/06/62	Owen Racing Organisation	BRM P57-V8	engine
3	International 2000 Guineas	Mallory Park	11/06/62	Rob Walker	Lotus 18/21-Climax	
2	GT Race–Qual. Heat 3	Mallory Park	11/06/62	John Coombs	Jaguar E-type	
2	GT Race–Final	Mallory Park	11/06/62	John Coombs	Jaguar E-type	
2	**BELGIAN GP**	Spa	17/06/62	Owen Racing Organisation	BRM P57-V8	Pole
ret	Le Mans 24 Hours	Le Mans	23-24/06/62	David Brown	Aston Martin 4 litre	c/d Ginther/oil pipe
2	Reims GP	Reims	01/07/62	Owen Racing Organisation	BRM P57-V8	
9/ret	**FRENCH GP**	Rouen	08/07/62	Owen Racing Organisation	BRM P57-V8	delayed – fuel injection/Fastest lap
1	Scott-Brown Memorial	Snetterton	15/07/62	UDT-Laystall	Lotus 19-Climax	
1	Saloon Car Race	Snetterton	15/07/62	John Coombs	Jaguar Mk II 3.8	
4	**BRITISH GP**	Aintree	21/07/62	Owen Racing Organisation	BRM P57-V8	
1	**GERMAN GP**	Nürburgring	05/08/62	Owen Racing Organisation	BRM P57-V8	Fastest lap
4	Peco Trophy Race	Brands Hatch	06/08/62	John Coombs	Jaguar E-type	
ret	Saloon Car Race	Brands Hatch	06/08/62	John Coombs	Jaguar Mk II 3.8	crashed at Druids
ret	Kanonloppet	Karlskoga	12/08/62	Rob Walker	Lotus 18/21-Climax	oil leak
2	Tourist Trophy	Goodwood	18/08/62	John Coombs	Ferrari 250GTO	
1	Touring Car Race	Oulton Park	01/09/62	John Coombs	Jaguar Mk II 3.8	
2	Gold Cup	Oulton Park	01/09/62	Owen Racing Organisation	BRM P57-V8	
1	**ITALIAN GP**	Monza	16/09/62	Owen Racing Organisation	BRM P57-V8	Fastest lap
2	**US GP**	Watkins Glen	07/10/62	Owen Racing Organisation	BRM P57-V8	
ret	Riverside GP	Riverside	14/10/62	Bill Sturgis	Cooper T61-Monaco	gear linkage
ret	Pacific GP	Laguna Seca	21/10/62	Bill Sturgis	Cooper T61-Monaco	gearbox
ret	Rand GP	Kyalami	15/12/62	Owen Racing Organisation	BRM P57-V8	
2	Natal GP–Qual. Heat 1	Westmead	22/12/62	Owen Racing Organisation	BRM P57-V8	
15	Natal GP–Final	Westmead	22/12/62	Owen Racing Organisation	BRM P57-V8	ignition trouble
1	**SOUTH AFRICAN GP**	East London	29/12/62	Owen Racing Organisation	BRM P57-V8	

1963

ret	New Zealand GP	Pukekohe	05/01/63	Rob Walker	Ferguson P99 4WD	gearbox
6	Australian GP	Warwick Farm	10/02/63	Rob Walker	Ferguson P99 4WD	carburation
2	Lakeside International Trophy	Lakeside	17/02/63	Rob Walker	Ferguson P99 4WD	
ret	Sebring 3 Hours	Sebring	22/03/63	Speedwell Racing	MG Midget	axle
3	Sebring 12 Hours	Sebring	23/03/63	NART	Ferrari 330LM/SP	c/d P. Rodriguez
1	Lombank Trophy	Snetterton	30/03/63	Owen Racing Organisation	BRM P57-V8	
1	GT Race	Snetterton	30/03/63	John Coombs	Jaguar E-type	
2	Touring Car Race	Snetterton	30/03/63	John Coombs	Jaguar Mk II 3.8	
1	Touring Car Race	Oulton Park	06/04/63	John Coombs	Jaguar Mk II 3.8	
1	St Mary's Trophy	Goodwood	15/04/63	John Coombs	Jaguar Mk II 3.8	
1	Sussex Trophy	Goodwood	15/04/63	John Coombs	Jaguar E-type	
9	Glover Trophy	Goodwood	15/04/63	Owen Racing Organisation	BRM P57-V8	
1	Aintree '200'	Aintree	27/04/63	Owen Racing Organisation	BRM P57-V8	
1	Touring Car Race	Aintree	27/04/63	John Coombs	Jaguar Mk II 3.8	
1	GT Race	Silverstone	11/05/63	John Coombs	Jaguar E-type	
ret	Daily Express International Trophy	Silverstone	11/05/63	Owen Racing Organisation	BRM P57-V8	
1	**MONACO GP**	Monte Carlo	26/05/63	Owen Racing Organisation	BRM P57-V8	
ret	Player's 200	Mosport Park	01/06/63	British Racing Partnership	Lotus 19-Climax	holed piston
3	Saloon Car Race	Crystal Palace	03/06/63	John Coombs	Jaguar Mk II 3.8	
ret	**BELGIAN GP**	Spa	09/06/63	Owen Racing Organisation	BRM P57-V8	gearbox/Pole
n/c*	Le Mans 24 Hours	Le Mans	15-16/06/63	Owen Racing Organisation	Rover-BRM turbine	c/d Ginther/7th on road
ret	**DUTCH GP**	Zandvoort	23/06/63	Owen Racing Organisation	BRM P57-V8	overheating

Pos	Race	Circuit	Date	Entrant	Car	Notes
3	**FRENCH GP**	Reims	30/06/63	Owen Racing Organisation	BRM P61-V8	push-start–1 min. penalty
1	Grovewood Trophy	Mallory Park	13/07/63	John Coombs	Jaguar E-type	
3	**BRITISH GP**	Silverstone	20/07/63	Owen Racing Organisation	BRM P61-V8	out of fuel last lap
ret	**GERMAN GP**	Nürburgring	04/08/63	Owen Racing Organisation	BRM P61-V8	gearbox
ret	Guards Trophy	Brands Hatch	05/08/63	Maranello Concessionaires	Ferrari GTO	sheared throttle pedal
2	Molyslip Trophy 'B'	Brands Hatch	05/08/63	John Coombs	Jaguar E-type	
1	Tourist Trophy	Goodwood	24/08/63	Maranello Concessionaires	Ferrari GTO	
2*	Canadian GP	Mosport Park	28/08/63	Ian Walker	Lotus 23B-Climax	*1st in class
3	Northwest GP – Heat 1	Kent, Seattle	29/08/63	Winkelmann Racing	Lotus 23B-Climax	
ret	Northwest GP – Heat 2	Kent, Seattle	29/08/63	Winkelmann Racing	Lotus 23B-Climax	gearbox
ret	**ITALIAN GP**	Monza	08/09/63	Owen Racing Organisation	BRM P61-V8	clutch
2	Saloon Car Race	Oulton Park	21/09/63	John Willment	Ford Galaxie	
3	Gold Cup	Oulton Park	21/09/63	Owen Racing Organisation	BRM P57-V8	
1	**US GP**	Watkins Glen	06/10/63	Owen Racing Organisation	BRM P57-V8	Pole
10*	Riverside GP	Riverside	13/10/63	Ian Walker	Lotus 23B-Climax	*4th in class
12*	Monterey Pacific GP	Laguna Seca	20/10/63	Ian Walker	Lotus 23B-Climax	*4th in class
4	**MEXICAN GP**	Mexico City	27/10/63	Owen Racing Organisation	BRM P57-V8	
3	**SOUTH AFRICAN GP**	East London	28/12/63	Owen Racing Organisation	BRM P57-V8	

1964

Pos	Race	Circuit	Date	Entrant	Car	Notes
4	International 100	Warwick Farm	16/02/64	Scuderia Veloce	Brabham BT3-Climax	
1	South Pacific Trophy	Longford	02/03/64	Scuderia Veloce	Brabham BT3-Climax	
ret	*Daily Mirror* Trophy	Snetterton	14/03/64	Owen Racing Organisation	BRM P261-V8	lost wheel–crashed
ret	Sebring 12 Hours	Sebring	21/03/64	Maranello Concessionaires	4.0 Ferrari 330	c/d Bonnier/gearbox
ret	*News of the World* Trophy	Goodwood	30/03/64	Owen Racing Organisation	BRM P261-V8	rotor arm
1	Sussex Trophy	Goodwood	30/03/64	Maranello Concessionaires	3.0 Ferrari GTO	
dns	Pau GP	Pau	05/04/64	Jean Redélé	Alpine-Renault F2	car not raceworthy
2	Aintree 200	Aintree	18/04/64	Owen Racing Organisation	BRM P261-V8	
ret	Targa Florio	Madonie Circuit	26/04/64	Maranello Concessionaires	2.0 Ferrari P2	c/d Bonnier/halfshaft
1	GT Race	Silverstone	02/05/64	Maranello Concessionaires	3.0 Ferrari GTO	
2	*Daily Express* International Trophy	Silverstone	02/05/64	Owen Racing Organisation	BRM P261-V8	
1	**MONACO GP**	Monte Carlo	10/05/64	Owen Racing Organisation	BRM P261-V8	Fastest lap
1	London Trophy – Heat 1	Crystal Palace	18/05/64	John Coombs	Cooper T72-Cosworth F2	
2	London Trophy – Final	Crystal Palace	18/05/64	John Coombs	Cooper T72-Cosworth F2	
4	**DUTCH GP**	Zandvoort	24/05/64	Owen Racing Organisation	BRM P261-V8	c/d Ireland/refuelled on circuit
dsq	Nürburgring 1000 Km	Nürburgring	31/05/64	Maranello Concessionaires	3.3 Ferrari 275P	c/d Bonnier
1	Reims 12 Hours	Reims	05/06/64	Maranello Concessionaires	3.3 Ferrari 250LM	out of fuel last lap
5/ret	**BELGIAN GP**	Spa	14/06/64	Owen Racing Organisation	BRM P261-V8	c/d Bonnier
2	Le Mans 24 Hours	Le Mans	20-21/06/64	Maranello Concessionaires	4.0 Ferrari 330P3	
2	**FRENCH GP**	Rouen	28/06/64	Owen Racing Organisation	BRM P261-V8	
ret	Reims GP	Reims	05/07/64	John Coombs	Brabham BT10-Cosworth F2	
2	**BRITISH GP**	Brands Hatch	11/07/64	Owen Racing Organisation	BRM P261/V8	
ret	Solitude GP	Solitude	19/07/64	Owen Racing Organisation	BRM P261-V8	spun off/wet track
2	**GERMAN GP**	Nürburgring	02/08/64	Owen Racing Organisation	BRM P261-V8	
3	British Eagle Trophy	Brands Hatch	03/08/64	John Coombs	Brabham BT10-Cosworth F2	
4	Guards International Trophy	Brands Hatch	03/08/64	Maranello Concessionaires	4.0 Ferrari 330P	
ret	**AUSTRIAN GP**	Zeltweg	23/08/64	Owen Racing Organisation	BRM P261-V8	distributor drive/Pole
1	Tourist Trophy	Goodwood	29/08/64	Maranello Concessionaires	4.0 Ferrari 330P	
ret	**ITALIAN GP**	Monza	06/09/64	Owen Racing Organisation	BRM P261-V8	clutch at start
ret	Gold Cup	Oulton Park	19/09/64	John Coombs	Brabham BT10-Cosworth F2	engine
ret	*Autosport* 3 Hours	Snetterton	26/09/64	Maranello Concessionaires	Ferrari 250LM	oil pressure
9	Grand Prix de l'Ile de France	Montlhéry	27/09/64	John Coombs	Brabham BT10-Cosworth F2	brakes
1	**US GP**	Watkins Glen	04/10/64	Owen Racing Organisation	BRM P261-V8	
1	Paris 1000 Km	Montlhéry	11/10/64	Maranello Concessionaires	Ferrari 330P	c/d Bonnier
11	**MEXICAN GP**	Mexico City	25/10/64	Owen Racing Organisation	BRM P261-V8	shunted by Bandini
1	Rand GP – Heat 1	Kyalami	12/12/64	John Willment	Brabham BT11-BRM V8	
1	Rand GP – Heat 2	Kyalami	12/12/64	John Willment	Brabham BT11-BRM V8	1st on aggregate

1965

Pos	Race	Circuit	Date	Entrant	Car	Notes
3	**SOUTH AFRICAN GP**	East London	01/01/65	Owen Racing Organisation	BRM P261-V8	
1	Preliminary Heat 2	Pukekohe	09/01/65	Scuderia Veloce	Brabham BT3-Climax	
1	New Zealand GP	Pukekohe	09/01/65	Scuderia Veloce	Brabham BT3-Climax	Fastest lap
5	International 100	Warwick Farm	14/02/65	Scuderia Veloce	Brabham BT3-Climax	steering problem
ret	International Cup	Sandown Park	21/02/65	Scuderia Veloce	Brabham BT3-Climax	cylinder head
1	*Launceston Examiner* Race	Longford	27/02/65	Scuderia Veloce	Brabham BT3-Climax	

1965 continued

4	Australian GP	Longford	03/03/65	Scuderia Veloce	Brabham BT3-Climax	
5	Race of Champions – Heat 1	Brands Hatch	13/03/65	Owen Racing Organisation	BRM P261-V8	
ret	Race of Champions – Heat 2	Brands Hatch	13/03/65	Owen Racing Organisation	BRM P261-V8	overheating
ret	Sports Car Race	Silverstone	20/03/65	John Coombs	McLaren Elva-Oldsmobile	engine
ret	Sebring 12 Hours	Sebring	27/03/65	John Mecom	Ferrari 330P	c/d P. Rodriguez/clutch
ret	Daily Express Cup	Oulton Park	03/04/65	John Coombs	Brabham BT16-BRM F2	engine
1	Autocar Trophy – Heat 1	Snetterton	10/04/65	John Coombs	Brabham BT16-BRM F2	
1	Autocar Trophy – Heat 2	Snetterton	10/04/65	John Coombs	Brabham BT16-BRM F2	1st on aggregate
2	Sunday Mirror Trophy	Goodwood	19/04/65	Owen Racing Organisation	BRM P261-V8	
ret	Pau GP	Pau	25/04/65	John Coombs	Brabham BT16-BRM F2	seized engine
1	Guards Trophy – Heat 1	Mallory Park	06/05/65	John Coombs	McLaren Elva-Oldsmobile	
dns	Guards Trophy – Heat 2	Mallory Park	06/05/65	John Coombs	McLaren Elva-Oldsmobile	engine trouble
4	Targa Florio	Madonie Circuit	09/05/65	Porsche System Engineering	Porsche F8 Coupé	c/d Bonnier
ret	Daily Express International Trophy	Silverstone	15/05/65	Owen Racing Organisation	BRM P261-V8	camshaft
ret	Nürburgring 1000 Km	Nürburgring	23/05/65	Maranello Concessionaires	3.3 Ferrari 275P2	c/d Stewart/electrics
1	**MONACO GP**	Monte Carlo	30/05/65	Owen Racing Organisation	BRM P261-V8	Pole/Fastest lap
2	London Trophy – Heat 1	Crystal Palace	07/06/65	John Coombs	Brabham BT16-BRM F2	
2	London Trophy – Heat 2	Crystal Palace	07/06/65	John Coombs	Brabham BT16-BRM F2	2nd on aggregate
5	**BELGIAN GP**	Spa	13/06/65	Owen Racing Organisation	BRM P261-V8	Pole
10	Le Mans 24 Hours	Le Mans	19-20/06/65	Owen Racing Organisation	2.0 Rover-BRM turbine	c/d Stewart
5	**FRENCH GP**	Clermont-Ferrand	27/06/65	Owen Racing Organisation	BRM P261-V8	
ret	Reims GP	Reims	03/07/65	John Coombs	Brabham BT16-BRM F2	engine
11	Reims 12 Hours	Reims	03-04/07/65	Maranello Concessionaires	4.0 Ferrari 330P2	c/d Bonnier/gear trouble
2	**BRITISH GP**	Silverstone	10/07/65	Owen Racing Organisation	BRM P261-V8	Fastest lap
2	Rouen GP	Rouen	11/07/65	John Coombs	Brabham BT16-BMW F2	
4	**DUTCH GP**	Zandvoort	18/07/65	Owen Racing Organisation	BRM P261-V8	Pole
2	**GERMAN GP**	Nürburgring	01/08/65	Owen Racing Organisation	BRM P261-V8	
ret	Kanonloppet	Karlskoga	08/08/65	John Coombs	Brabham BT16-BMW F2	
nc	Guards International Trophy – Heat 1	Brands Hatch	30/08/65	John Coombs	McLaren Elva-Oldsmobile	
nc	Guards International Trophy – Heat 2	Brands Hatch	30/08/65	John Coombs	McLaren Elva-Oldsmobile	
4	British Eagle Trophy	Brands Hatch	30/08/65	John Coombs	Lotus 35-BRM F2	
2	**ITALIAN GP**	Monza	12/09/65	Owen Racing Organisation	BRM P261-V8	
3	Gold Cup	Oulton Park	18/09/65	John Coombs	Lotus 35-BRM F2	raced Ron Harris spare car
ret	Albi GP	Albi	26/09/65	John Coombs	Lotus 35-BRM F2	fuel pump
1	**US GP**	Watkins Glen	03/10/65	Owen Racing Organisation	BRM P261-V8	Pole/Fastest lap
ret	**MEXICAN GP**	Mexico City	24/10/65	Owen Racing Organisation	BRM P261-V8	broken con rod
ret	Times GP	Riverside	31/10/65		McLaren Elva-Oldsmobile	lost wheel

1966

1	New Zealand GP	Pukekohe	08/01/66	Owen Racing Organisation	BRM P261T-V8	
2	International 100	Warwick Farm	13/02/66	Owen Racing Organisation	BRM P261T-V8	
1	Australian GP	Lakeside	20/02/66	Owen Racing Organisation	BRM P261T-V8	
3	Exide International 100	Sandown Park	27/02/66	Owen Racing Organisation	BRM P261T-V8	
2	Launceston Examiner Race	Longford	05/03/66	Owen Racing Organisation	BRM P261T-V8	
2	South Pacific Trophy	Longford	07/03/66	Owen Racing Organisation	BRM P261T-V8	
ret	Sebring 12 Hours	Sebring	26/03/66	Alan Mann Racing	Ford GT40	c/d Stewart/fire after spin
dns	BARC 200	Oulton Park	02/04/66	John Coombs	Brabham BT16-BRM F2	race day snowed off
ret	Archie Scott-Brown Trophy	Snetterton	08/04/66	Team Surtees	Lola T70-Chevrolet V8	final drive
5	Sunday Mirror Trophy	Goodwood	11/04/66	John Coombs	Brabham BT16-BRM F2	
3	Pau GP	Pau	17/04/66	John Coombs	Brabham BT16-BRM F2	
6	Juan Jover Trophy	Barcelona	25/04/66	John Coombs	Brabham BT16-BRM F2	
ret	Limbourg GP	Zolder	08/05/66	John Coombs	Matra MS5-BRM F2	
3	**MONACO GP**	Monte Carlo	22/05/66	Owen Racing Organisation	BRM P261-V8 2 litre	
1	Indianapolis 500	Indianapolis	30/05/66	John Mecom	Lola T90-Ford 4.2 litre	
ret	**BELGIAN GP**	Spa	12/06/66	Owen Racing Organisation	BRM P261-V8 2 litre	spun off
ret	Le Mans 24 Hours	Le Mans	18-19/06/66	Alan Mann	Ford Mk II prototype	c/d Muir/front suspension
11/ret	Reims GP	Reims	02/07/66	John Coombs	Matra MS5-BRM F2	
ret	**FRENCH GP**	Reims	03/07/66	Owen Racing Organisation	BRM P261-V8 2 litre	camshaft
5	Rouen GP	Rouen	10/07/66	John Coombs	Matra MS5-BRM F2	
3	**BRITISH GP**	Brands Hatch	16/07/66	Owen Racing Organisation	BRM P261-V8 2 litre	
2	**DUTCH GP**	Zandvoort	24/07/66	Owen Racing Organisation	BRM P261-V8 2 litre	
4	**GERMAN GP**	Nürburgring	07/08/66	Owen Racing Organisation	BRM P261-V8 2 litre	
3	Guards International Trophy	Brands Hatch	29/08/66	Team Surtees	Lola T70 Mk 2-Chevrolet V8	
ret	**ITALIAN GP**	Monza	04/09/66	Owen Racing Organisation	BRM T83-H16 3 litre	engine
8	GP de l'Ile de France	Montlhéry	11/09/66	John Coombs	Matra MS5-BRM F2	
ret	Gold Cup	Oulton Park	17/09/66	Owen Racing Organisation	BRM T83-H16 3 litre	camshaft
ret	Trophée Craven A	Le Mans	18/09/66	John Coombs	Matra MS5-BRM F2	camshaft
10	Albi GP	Albi	25/09/66	John Coombs	Matra MS5-BRM F2	
ret	**US GP**	Watkins Glen	02/10/66	Owen Racing Organisation	BRM T83-H16 3 litre	gearbox
5/ret	Mt Fuji Race	Fuji Speedway	09/10/66	John Mecom	Lola T90-Ford 4.2 litre	
3	Los Angeles Times GP	Riverside	30/10/66	Team Surtees	Lola T70 Mk 2-Chevrolet V8	

1967

ret	**SOUTH AFRICAN GP**	Kyalami	02/01/67	Team Lotus	Lotus 43-BRM H16	*suspension*
ret	Australian GP	Warwick Farm	19/02/67	Team Lotus	Lotus 48-Cosworth F2	*transmission*
2*	Lombank Trophy	Brands Hatch	12/03/67	Team Lotus	Lotus-Ford Cortina	**1st up to 2-litre class*
2	Guards 100	Snetterton	24/03/67	Team Lotus	Lotus 48-Cosworth F2	
ret	Wills Trophy – Heat 1	Silverstone	27/03/67	Team Lotus	Lotus 48-Cosworth F2	
2	Wills Trophy – Heat 2	Silverstone	27/03/67	Team Lotus	Lotus 48-Cosworth F2	
ret	Pau GP	Pau	02/04/67	Team Lotus	Lotus 48-Cosworth F2	*gearbox*
ret	Juan Jover Trophy	Barcelona	09/04/67	Team Lotus	Lotus 48-Cosworth F2	*metering unit*
8	Spring Cup	Oulton Park	15/04/67	Team Lotus	Lotus 48-Cosworth F2	
15	Eifelrennen	Nürburgring	23/04/67	Team Lotus	Lotus 48-Cosworth F2	
4	*Daily Express* International Trophy	Silverstone	29/04/67	Team Lotus	Lotus 33-BRM V12 2 litre	
2	**MONACO GP**	Monte Carlo	07/05/67	Team Lotus	Lotus 33-BRM V12 2 litre	
ret	Indianapolis 500	Indianapolis	30-31/05/67	STP-Team Lotus	Lotus 42F-Ford 4.2 litre	*piston*
ret	**DUTCH GP**	Zandvoort	04/06/67	Team Lotus	Lotus 49-Cosworth V8	*timing gears/Pole*
ret	**BELGIAN GP**	Spa	18/06/67	Team Lotus	Lotus 49-Cosworth V8	*gearbox*
2	Reims GP	Reims	25/06/67	Team Lotus	Lotus 48-Cosworth F2	
ret	**FRENCH GP**	Le Mans	02/07/67	Team Lotus	Lotus 49-Cosworth V8	*gearbox/Pole/Fastest lap*
4	Rouen GP	Rouen	09/07/67	Team Lotus	Lotus 48-Cosworth F2	
ret	**BRITISH GP**	Silverstone	15/07/67	Team Lotus	Lotus 49-Cosworth V8	*engine*
6	Flugplatzrennen	Tulln Langenlebarn	16/07/67	Team Lotus	Lotus 48-Cosworth F2	
ret	Madrid GP	Jarama	23/07/67	Team Lotus	Lotus 48-Cosworth F2	*electrics*
ret	BOAC 500	Brands Hatch	30/07/67	Porsche System Engineering	Porsche 910 F8	*c/d Rindt/dropped valve*
ret	**GERMAN GP**	Nürburgring	06/08/67	Team Lotus	Lotus 49-Cosworth V8	*suspension*
5	Swedish GP	Karlskoga	13/08/67	Team Lotus	Lotus 48-Cosworth F2	
7	Mediterranean GP	Enna-Pergusa	20/08/67	Team Lotus	Lotus 48-Cosworth F2	
4	**CANADIAN GP**	Mosport Park	27/08/67	Team Lotus	Lotus 49-Cosworth V8	
7	Guards Trophy	Brands Hatch	28/08/67	Team Lotus	Lotus 48-Cosworth F2	
3	Suomen GP	Keimola	03/09/67	Team Lotus	Lotus 48-Cosworth F2	
5	Hämeenlinnan Ajot	Ahvenisto	05/09/67	Team Lotus	Lotus 48-Cosworth F2	
ret	**ITALIAN GP**	Monza	10/09/67	Team Lotus	Lotus 49-Cosworth V8	*engine*
2	Gold Cup	Oulton Park	17/09/67	Team Lotus	Lotus 48-Cosworth F2	
ret	Albi GP	Albi	24/09/67	Team Lotus	Lotus 48-Cosworth F2	
2	**US GP**	Watkins Glen	01/10/67	Team Lotus	Lotus 49-Cosworth V8	*Pole/Fastest lap*
8	Rome GP	Vallelunga	08/10/67	Team Lotus	Lotus 48-Cosworth F2	
ret	**MEXICAN GP**	Mexico City	22/10/67	Team Lotus	Lotus 49-Cosworth V8	*broken u-joint*
2	Spanish GP	Jarama	12/11/67	Team Lotus	Lotus 49-Cosworth V8	

1968

2	**SOUTH AFRICAN GP**	Kyalami	01/01/68	Team Lotus	Lotus 49-Cosworth V8	
2	Rothmans International 100	Surfer's Paradise	11/02/68	Gold Leaf Team Lotus	Lotus 49T-Cosworth V8	
2	International 100	Warwick Farm	18/02/68	Gold Leaf Team Lotus	Lotus 49T-Cosworth V8	
3	Australian GP	Sandown Park	25/02/68	Gold Leaf Team Lotus	Lotus 49T-Cosworth V8	
6	South Pacific Trophy	Longford	04/03/68	Gold Leaf Team Lotus	Lotus 49T-Cosworth V8	
ret	Race of Champions	Brands Hatch	17/03/68	Gold Leaf Team Lotus	Lotus 49-Cosworth V8	*broken driveshaft*
ret	Juan Jover Trophy	Barcelona	31/03/68	Gold Leaf Team Lotus	Lotus 48-Cosworth F2	*engine*
12	Deutschland Trophy – Heat 1	Hockenheim	07/04/68	Gold Leaf Team Lotus	Lotus 48-Cosworth F2	
dns	Deutschland Trophy – Heat 2	Hockenheim	07/04/68	Gold Leaf Team Lotus	Lotus 48-Cosworth F2	*car withdrawn*
ret	*Daily Express* International Trophy	Silverstone	20/04/68	Gold Leaf Team Lotus	Lotus 49-Cosworth V8	*fuel line*
ret	Gran Premio de Madrid	Jarama	28/04/68	Gold Leaf Team Lotus	Lotus 48-Cosworth F2	*broken wheel studs*
1	**SPANISH GP**	Jarama	12/05/68	Gold Leaf Team Lotus	Lotus 49-Cosworth V8	
1	**MONACO GP**	Monte Carlo	26/05/68	Gold Leaf Team Lotus	Lotus 49B-Cosworth V8	*Pole*
ret	Indianapolis 500	Indianapolis	30/05/68	STP-Team Lotus	STP-Lotus 56 turbine	*spun into wall*
9/ret	Holts Trophy	Crystal Palace	28/05/68	Gold Leaf Team Lotus	Lotus 48-Cosworth F2	*lost wheel*
ret	**BELGIAN GP**	Spa	09/06/68	Gold Leaf Team Lotus	Lotus 49B-Cosworth V8	*broken u-joint*
dns	Canadian Telegram Trophy	Mosport Park	15/06/68	STP-Team Lotus	STP-Lotus 56 turbine	*practice accident*
9/ret	**DUTCH GP**	Zandvoort	23/06/68	Gold Leaf Team Lotus	Lotus 49B-Cosworth V8	*spun off*
ret	**FRENCH GP**	Rouen	07/07/68	Gold Leaf Team Lotus	Lotus 49B-Cosworth V8	*driveshaft*
ret	OAMTC Flugplatzrennen	Tulln Langenlebarn	14/07/68	Gold Leaf Team Lotus	Lotus 48-Cosworth F2	*gearbox oil leak*
ret	**BRITISH GP**	Brands Hatch	20/07/68	Gold Leaf Team Lotus	Lotus 49B-Cosworth V8	*broken u-joint/Pole*
2	**GERMAN GP**	Nürburgring	04/08/68	Gold Leaf Team Lotus	Lotus 49B-Cosworth V8	
ret	Gold Cup	Oulton Park	17/08/68	Gold Leaf Team Lotus	Lotus 49B-Cosworth V8	*c.w. pinion*
ret	Saloon Car Race	Oulton Park	17/08/68	Alan Mann	Ford Escort-FVA	*puncture*
ret	**ITALIAN GP**	Monza	08/09/68	Gold Leaf Team Lotus	Lotus 49B-Cosworth V8	*sheared wheel*
4	Trophées de France	Reims	15/09/68	Gold Leaf Team Lotus	Lotus 48-Cosworth F2	
4	**CANADIAN GP**	Mont Tremblant	22/09/68	Gold Leaf Team Lotus	Lotus 49B-Cosworth V8	
2	**US GP**	Watkins Glen	06/10/68	Gold Leaf Team Lotus	Lotus 49B-Cosworth V8	

1968 continued

14/ret	Grand Prix d'Albi	Albi	20/10/68	Gold Leaf Team Lotus	Lotus 48-Cosworth F2	brake caliper seal
7	Rome GP – Heat 1	Vallelunga	27/10/68	Gold Leaf Team Lotus	Lotus 48-Cosworth F2	
7	Rome GP – Heat 2	Vallelunga	27/10/68	Gold Leaf Team Lotus	Lotus 48-Cosworth F2	7th on aggregate
1	**MEXICAN GP**	Mexico City	03/11/68	Gold Leaf Team Lotus	Lotus 49B-Cosworth V8	

1969

ret	New Zealand GP	Pukekohe	04/01/69	Gold Leaf Team Lotus	Lotus 49T-Cosworth V8	suspension
ret	Rothmans International 100	Levin	11/01/69	Gold Leaf Team Lotus	Lotus 49T-Cosworth V8	driveshaft
1	Preliminary Heat 2	Christchurch	18/01/69	Gold Leaf Team Lotus	Lotus 49T-Cosworth V8	
2	Lady Wigram Trophy	Christchurch	18/01/69	Gold Leaf Team Lotus	Lotus 49T-Cosworth V8	
6	Preliminary Heat 1	Invercargill	25/01/69	Gold Leaf Team Lotus	Lotus 49T-Cosworth V8	
2	Rothmans International 100	Invercargill	25/01/69	Gold Leaf Team Lotus	Lotus 49T-Cosworth V8	
4	Australian GP	Lakeside	02/02/69	Gold Leaf Team Lotus	Lotus 49T-Cosworth V8	
11	International Tasman 100	Warwick Farm	09/02/69	Gold Leaf Team Lotus	Lotus 49T-Cosworth V8	
6	Sandown Park International	Sandown Park	16/02/69	Gold Leaf Team Lotus	Lotus 49T-Cosworth V8	
2	**SOUTH AFRICAN GP**	Kyalami	01/03/69	Gold Leaf Team Lotus	Lotus 49B-Cosworth V8	
2	Race of Champions	Brands Hatch	19/03/69	Gold Leaf Team Lotus	Lotus 49B-Cosworth V8	
7	Daily Express International Trophy	Silverstone	30/03/69	Gold Leaf Team Lotus	Lotus 49B-Cosworth V8	
3	Wills Trophy – Heat 1	Thruxton	07/04/69	Roy Winkelmann Racing	Lotus 59B-Cosworth F2	
ret	Wills Trophy – Final	Thruxton	07/04/69	Roy Winkelmann Racing	Lotus 59B-Cosworth F2	clutch
ret	Pau GP	Pau	20/04/69	Roy Winkelmann Racing	Lotus 59B-Cosworth F2	metering belt to fuel injection
ret	ADAC Eifelrennen	Nürburgring	27/04/69	Roy Winkelmann Racing	Lotus 59B-Cosworth F2	broken front wishbone
ret	**SPANISH GP**	Barcelona	04/05/69	Gold Leaf Team Lotus	Lotus 49B-Cosworth V8	aerofoil collapsed–crashed
1	**MONACO GP**	Monte Carlo	18/05/69	Gold Leaf Team Lotus	Lotus 49B-Cosworth V8	
2	Limbourg GP – Heat 1	Zolder	08/06/69	Roy Winkelmann Racing	Lotus 48-Cosworth F2	
ret	Limbourg GP – Heat 2	Zolder	08/06/69	Roy Winkelmann Racing	Lotus 48-Cosworth F2	rear suspension
7	**DUTCH GP**	Zandvoort	21/06/69	Gold Leaf Team Lotus	Lotus 49B-Cosworth V8	
ret	Trophées de France	Reims	29/06/69	Roy Winkelmann Racing	Lotus 48-Cosworth F2	collision–Galli
6	**FRENCH GP**	Clermont-Ferrand	06/07/69	Gold Leaf Team Lotus	Lotus 49B-Cosworth V8	
3	Flugplatzrennen – Heat 1	Tulln Langenlebarn	13/07/69	Roy Winkelmann Racing	Lotus 48-Cosworth F2	
3	Flugplatzrennen – Heat 2	Tulln Langenlebarn	13/07/69	Roy Winkelmann Racing	Lotus 48-Cosworth F2	3rd on aggregate
7	**BRITISH GP**	Silverstone	19/07/69	Gold Leaf Team Lotus	Lotus 49B-Cosworth V8	
4	**GERMAN GP**	Nürburgring	03/08/69	Gold Leaf Team Lotus	Lotus 49B-Cosworth V8	
ret	Gold Cup	Oulton Park	16/08/69	Roy Winkelmann Racing	Lotus 59B-Cosworth F2	oil pressure gauge pipe
7	Enna GP – Heat 1	Enna-Pergusa	24/08/69	Roy Winkelmann Racing	Lotus 59B-Cosworth F2	clutch trouble
2	Enna GP – Heat 2	Enna-Pergusa	24/08/69	Roy Winkelmann Racing	Lotus 59B-Cosworth F2	6th on aggregate
9/ret	**ITALIAN GP**	Monza	07/09/69	Gold Leaf Team Lotus	Lotus 49B-Cosworth V8	driveshaft
1	Albi GP	Albi	14/09/69	Roy Winkelmann Racing	Lotus 59B-Cosworth F2	
ret	**CANADIAN GP**	Mosport Park	20/09/69	Gold Leaf Team Lotus	Lotus 49B-Cosworth V8	camshaft
ret	**US GP**	Watkins Glen	05/10/69	Gold Leaf Team Lotus	Lotus 49B-Cosworth V8	tyre deflated–crashed

1970

6	**SOUTH AFRICAN GP**	Kyalami	07/03/70	Rob Walker Racing Team	Lotus 49C-Cosworth V8	
4	Race of Champions	Brands Hatch	22/03/70	Rob Walker Racing Team	Lotus 49C-Cosworth V8	
4	**SPANISH GP**	Jarama	19/04/70	Rob Walker Racing Team	Lotus 49C-Cosworth V8	
14	Daily Express International Trophy – Heat 1	Silverstone	26/04/70	Rob Walker Racing Team	Lotus 49C-Cosworth V8	pit stop
4	Daily Express International Trophy – Heat 2	Silverstone	26/04/70	Rob Walker Racing Team	Lotus 49C-Cosworth V8	9th on aggregate
5	**MONACO GP**	Monte Carlo	10/05/70	Brooke Bond Oxo Racing/Rob Walker	Lotus 49C-Cosworth V8	
9	Ford Capri 3000 GT Race	Brands Hatch	24/05/70	Ford Motor Company	Ford Capri 3000 GT	
4	Alcoa Trophy – Qual. Heat 1	Crystal Palace	25/05/70	Jochen Rindt Team Lotus	Lotus 69-Cosworth F2	
5	Alcoa Trophy – Final	Crystal Palace	25/05/70	Jochen Rindt Team Lotus	Lotus 69-Cosworth F2	
ret	**BELGIAN GP**	Spa	07/06/70	Brooke Bond Oxo Racing/Rob Walker	Lotus 49C-Cosworth V8	engine
ret	Rhine Cup	Hockenheim	14/06/70	Jochen Rindt Team Lotus	Lotus 69-Cosworth F2	belt to metering unit
12	**DUTCH GP**	Zandvoort	21/06/70	Brooke Bond Oxo Racing/Rob Walker	Lotus 49C-Cosworth V8	
8	Rouen GP – Qual. Heat 1	Rouen	28/06/70	Jochen Rindt Team Lotus	Lotus 69-Cosworth F2	
dnq	Rouen GP – Final	Rouen	28/06/70	Jochen Rindt Team Lotus	Lotus 69-Cosworth F2	
10	**FRENCH GP**	Clermont-Ferrand	05/07/70	Brooke Bond Oxo Racing/Rob Walker	Lotus 49C-Cosworth V8	
6	**BRITISH GP**	Brands Hatch	19/07/70	Brooke Bond Oxo Racing/Rob Walker	Lotus 49C-Cosworth V8	no clutch
5	Trophées de France	Paul Ricard	26/07/70	Jochen Rindt Racing Team	Lotus 69-Cosworth F2	
ret	**GERMAN GP**	Hockenheim	02/08/70	Brooke Bond Oxo Racing/Rob Walker	Lotus 49C-Cosworth V8	engine
18/ret	Gold Cup – Heat 1	Oulton Park	22/08/70	Brooke Bond Oxo Racing/Rob Walker	Lotus 72C-Cosworth V8	engine
5	Preis von Salzburg – Heat 1	Salzburgring	30/08/70	Jochen Rindt Racing Team	Lotus 69-Cosworth F2	
6	Preis von Salzburg – Heat 2	Salzburgring	30/08/70	Jochen Rindt Racing Team	Lotus 69-Cosworth F2	5th on aggregate
dns	**ITALIAN GP**	Monza	06/09/70	Brooke Bond Oxo Racing/Rob Walker	Lotus 72C-Cosworth V8	withdrawn after Rindt's accident
nc	**CANADIAN GP**	Mont Tremblant	20/09/70	Brooke Bond Oxo Racing/Rob Walker	Lotus 72C-Cosworth V8	pit stop – gearbox
ret	**US GP**	Watkins Glen	04/10/70	Brooke Bond Oxo Racing/Rob Walker	Lotus 72C-Cosworth V8	clutch
ret	**MEXICAN GP**	Mexico City	25/10/70	Brooke Bond Oxo Racing/Rob Walker	Lotus 72C-Cosworth V8	engine

1971

Pos	Race	Circuit	Date	Entrant	Car	Notes
3	Colombian GP – Heat 1	Bogota	04/02/71	Bernie Ecclestone	Lotus 69-Cosworth F2	
4	Colombian GP – Heat 2	Bogota	04/02/71	Bernie Ecclestone	Lotus 69-Cosworth F2	2nd on aggregate
ret	Bogota GP – Heat 1	Bogota	07/02/71	Bernie Ecclestone	Lotus 69-Cosworth F2	fuel metering unit
5	Bogota GP – Heat 2	Bogota	07/02/71	Bernie Ecclestone	Lotus 69-Cosworth F2	
9	SOUTH AFRICAN GP	Kyalami	06/03/71	Motor Racing Developments	Brabham BT33-Cosworth V8	
ret	Race of Champions	Brands Hatch	21/03/71	Motor Racing Developments	Brabham BT34-Cosworth V8	engine
ret	Questor GP – Heat 1	Ontario	28/03/71	Motor Racing Developments	Brabham BT34-Cosworth V8	broken oil line
3	Jim Clark Trophy – Heat 1	Hockenheim	04/04/71	Rondel Racing	Brabham BT36-Cosworth F2	
1	Jim Clark Trophy – Heat 2	Hockenheim	04/04/71	Rondel Racing	Brabham BT36-Cosworth F2	2nd on aggregate
1	Jochen Rindt Memorial Trophy – Heat 1	Thruxton	12/04/71	Rondel Racing	Brabham BT36-Cosworth F2	
1	Jochen Rindt Memorial Trophy – Final	Thruxton	12/04/71	Rondel Racing	Brabham BT36-Cosworth F2	
ret	SPANISH GP	Barcelona	18/04/71	Motor Racing Developments	Brabham BT34-Cosworth V8	steering
10/ret	Pau GP	Pau	25/04/71	Rondel Racing	Brabham BT36-Cosworth F2	water pump drive
5	ADAC Eifelrennen	Nürburgring	02/05/71	Rondel Racing	Brabham BT36-Cosworth F2	
3	Daily Express International Trophy – Heat 1	Silverstone	08/05/71	Motor Racing Developments	Brabham BT34-Cosworth V8	
1	Daily Express International Trophy – Heat 2	Silverstone	08/05/71	Motor Racing Developments	Brabham BT34-Cosworth V8	1st on aggregate
ret	MONACO GP	Monte Carlo	23/05/71	Motor Racing Developments	Brabham BT34-Cosworth V8	crashed
ret	Hilton Transport Trophy – Qual. Heat 1	Crystal Palace	31/05/71	Rondel Racing	Brabham BT36-Cosworth F2	metering unit
dnq	Hilton Transport Trophy – Final	Crystal Palace	31/05/71	Rondel Racing	Brabham BT36-Cosworth F2	
10	DUTCH GP	Zandvoort	20/06/71	Motor Racing Developments	Brabham BT34-Cosworth V8	
3	Rouen GP	Rouen	27/06/71	Rondel Racing	Brabham BT36-Cosworth F2	
ret	FRENCH GP	Paul Ricard	04/07/71	Motor Racing Developments	Brabham BT34-Cosworth V8	oil pressure
ret	BRITISH GP	Silverstone	17/07/71	Motor Racing Developments	Brabham BT34-Cosworth V8	hit by Oliver on grid
9	GERMAN GP	Nürburgring	01/08/71	Motor Racing Developments	Brabham BT34-Cosworth V8	left on grid
5	AUSTRIAN GP	Österreichring	15/08/71	Motor Racing Developments	Brabham BT34-Cosworth V8	
13	Swedish Gold Cup – Heat 1	Kinnekulle	22/08/71	Rondel Racing	Brabham BT36-Cosworth F2	
13	Swedish Gold Cup – Heat 2	Kinnekulle	22/08/71	Rondel Racing	Brabham BT36-Cosworth F2	14th on aggregate
2	Rothmans International Trophy	Brands Hatch	30/08/71	Rondel Racing	Brabham BT36-Cosworth F2	
11/ret	ITALIAN GP	Monza	05/09/71	Motor Racing Developments	Brabham BT34-Cosworth V8	seized gearbox
1	GT Race – Heat 1	Paul Ricard	12/09/71	Ford Britain	Ford Capri 3000 GT	c/d Surtees
ret	GT Race – Heat 2	Paul Ricard	12/09/71	Ford Britain	Ford Capri 3000 GT	c/d Surtees/transmission
ret	CANADIAN GP	Mosport Park	19/09/71	Motor Racing Developments	Brabham BT34-Cosworth V8	spun off
5	Albi GP	Albi	26/09/71	Rondel Racing	Brabham BT36-Cosworth F2	
7	US GP	Watkins Glen	03/10/71	Motor Racing Developments	Brabham BT34-Cosworth V8	
8	Rothmans Victory Race	Brands Hatch	24/10/71	Motor Racing Developments	Brabham BT34-Cosworth V8	
	TORNEIO F2 SERIES					
7	Round 1 – Heat 1	Interlagos	31/10/71	Rondel Racing	Brabham BT36-Cosworth F2	
4	Round 1 – Heat 2	Interlagos	31/10/71	Rondel Racing	Brabham BT36-Cosworth F2	6th on aggregate
9	Round 1 – Heat 1	Interlagos	07/11/71	Rondel Racing	Brabham BT36-Cosworth F2	
6	Round 2 – Heat 2	Interlagos	07/11/71	Rondel Racing	Brabham BT36-Cosworth F2	5th on aggregate
9	Round 3 – Heat 1	Cutyba	14/11/71	Rondel Racing	Brabham BT36-Cosworth F2	
5	Round 3 – Heat 2	Cutyba	14/11/71	Rondel Racing	Brabham BT36-Cosworth F2	6th on aggregate
14	Round 4 – Heat 1	Cordoba	21/11/71	Rondel Racing	Brabham BT36-Cosworth F2	
3	Round 4 – Heat 2	Cordoba	21/11/71	Rondel Racing	Brabham BT36-Cosworth F2	10th on aggregate

1972

Pos	Race	Circuit	Date	Entrant	Car	Notes
ret	ARGENTINE GP	Buenos Aires	23/01/72	Motor Racing Developments	Brabham BT33-Cosworth V8	fuel pump/tyres
6	SOUTH AFRICAN GP	Kyalami	04/03/72	Motor Racing Developments	Brabham BT33-Cosworth V8	
6	Esso Uniflo Trophy – Qual. Heat 2	Thruxton	03/04/72	Graham Hill/Tate of Leeds (Racing)	Brabham BT36-Cosworth F2	
ret	Esso Uniflo Trophy – Final	Thruxton	03/04/72	Graham Hill/Tate of Leeds (Racing)	Brabham BT36-Cosworth F2	engine
12	Jim Clark Trophy – Heat 1	Hockenheim	16/04/72	Jaegermeister Racing	Brabham BT36-Cosworth F2	
ret	Jim Clark Trophy – Heat 2	Hockenheim	16/04/72	Jaegermeister Racing	Brabham BT36-Cosworth F2	engine
7	International Trophy	Silverstone	23/04/72	Motor Racing Developments	Brabham BT37-Cosworth V8	
10	SPANISH GP	Jarama	01/05/72	Motor Racing Developments	Brabham BT37-Cosworth V8	
7	Pau GP – Qual. Heat 1	Pau	07/05/72	Jaegermeister Racing	Brabham BT38-Cosworth F2	
ret	Pau GP – Final	Pau	07/05/72	Jaegermeister Racing	Brabham BT38-Cosworth F2	split oil pipe
12	MONACO GP	Monte Carlo	14/05/72	Motor Racing Developments	Brabham BT37-Cosworth V8	
ret	Greater London Trophy – Qual. Heat 1	Crystal Palace	28/05/72	Jaegermeister Racing	Brabham BT38-Cosworth F2	collision–Birrell
dnq	Greater London Trophy – Final	Crystal Palace	28/05/72	Jaegermeister Racing	Brabham BT38-Cosworth F2	
1	Lottery GP – Heat 1	Monza	29/05/72	Jaegermeister Racing	Brabham BT38-Cosworth F2	
1	Lottery GP – Heat 2	Monza	29/05/72	Jaegermeister Racing	Brabham BT38-Cosworth F2	1st on aggregate
ret	BELGIAN GP	Nivelles	04/06/72	Motor Racing Developments	Brabham BT37-Cosworth V8	rear upright
1	Le Mans 24 Hours	Le Mans	10-11/06/72	Equipe Matra	Matra MS670-V12	c/d Pescarolo
8	Rouen GP – Qual. Heat 1	Rouen	25/06/72	Jaegermeister Racing	Brabham BT38-Cosworth F2	
7	Rouen GP – Final	Rouen	25/06/72	Jaegermeister Racing	Brabham BT38-Cosworth F2	
10	FRENCH GP	Clermont-Ferrand	02/07/72	Motor Racing Developments	Brabham BT37-Cosworth V8	
ret	BRITISH GP	Brands Hatch	15/07/72	Motor Racing Developments	Brabham BT37-Cosworth V8	crashed
11	Shell GP – Heat 1	Imola	23/07/72	Jaegermeister Racing	Brabham BT38-Cosworth F2	brake trouble
4	Shell GP – Heat 2	Imola	23/07/72	Jaegermeister Racing	Brabham BT38-Cosworth F2	5th on aggregate
6	GERMAN GP	Nürburgring	30/07/72	Motor Racing Developments	Brabham BT37-Cosworth V8	
ret	AUSTRIAN GP	Österreichring	13/08/72	Motor Racing Developments	Brabham BT37-Cosworth V8	fuel metering unit

1972 continued

4	Festival Prize – Heat 1	Salzburgring	03/09/72	Jaegermeister Racing	Brabham BT38-Cosworth F2
4	Festival Prize – Heat 2	Salzburgring	03/09/72	Jaegermeister Racing	Brabham BT38-Cosworth F2
5	**ITALIAN GP**	Monza	10/09/72	Motor Racing Developments	Brabham BT37-Cosworth V8
10	John Player F2 Race	Oulton Park	16/09/72	Jaegermeister Racing	Brabham BT38-Cosworth F2
8	**CANADIAN GP**	Mosport Park	24/09/72	Motor Racing Developments	Brabham BT37-Cosworth V8
5	Baden-Württemberg Prize	Hockenheim	01/10/72	Jaegermeister Racing	Brabham BT38-Cosworth F2
11	**US GP**	Watkins Glen	08/10/72	Motor Racing Developments	Brabham BT37-Cosworth V8
ret	John Player Trophy	Brands Hatch	22/10/72	Motor Racing Developments	Brabham BT37-Cosworth V8 *gear linkage*

1973

ret	Race of Champions	Brands Hatch	18/03/73	Motor Racing Developments	Brabham BT37-Cosworth V8 *collision–Pilette*
ret	**SPANISH GP**	Barcelona	29/04/73	Embassy Racing	Shadow DN1-Cosworth V8 *brakes*
ret	Spa 1000 Km	Spa	06/05/73	Matra Sports	Matra MS670-V12 *c/d Amon/Pescarolo/engine*
9	**BELGIAN GP**	Zolder	20/05/73	Embassy Racing	Shadow DN1-Cosworth V8
ret	**MONACO GP**	Monte Carlo	03/06/73	Embassy Racing	Shadow DN1-Cosworth V8 *rear suspension*
ret	**SWEDISH GP**	Anderstorp	17/06/73	Embassy Racing	Shadow DN1-Cosworth V8 *ignition*
10	**FRENCH GP**	Paul Ricard	01/07/73	Embassy Racing	Shadow DN1-Cosworth V8
ret	**BRITISH GP**	Silverstone	14/07/73	Embassy Racing	Shadow DN1-Cosworth V8 *loose steering rack*
nc	**DUTCH GP**	Zandvoort	29/07/73	Embassy Racing	Shadow DN1-Cosworth V8 *4 pit stops–water*
13	**GERMAN GP**	Nürburgring	05/08/73	Embassy Racing	Shadow DN1-Cosworth V8
ret	**AUSTRIAN GP**	Österreichring	19/08/73	Embassy Racing	Shadow DN1-Cosworth V8 *broken rear suspension*
14	**ITALIAN GP**	Monza	09/09/73	Embassy Racing	Shadow DN1-Cosworth V8
16	**CANADIAN GP**	Mosport Park	23/09/73	Embassy Racing	Shadow DN1-Cosworth V8 *4 pit stops*
13	**US GP**	Watkins Glen	07/10/73	Embassy Racing	Shadow DN1-Cosworth V8 *puncture*

1974

ret	**ARGENTINE GP**	Buenos Aires	13/01/74	Embassy Racing	Lola T370-Cosworth V8 *engine*
11	**BRAZILIAN GP**	Interlagos	27/01/74	Embassy Racing	Lola T370-Cosworth V8
nc	Race of Champions	Brands Hatch	17/03/74	Embassy Racing	Lola T370-Cosworth V8 *3 pit stops–17th place*
12	**SOUTH AFRICAN GP**	Kyalami	30/03/74	Embassy Racing	Lola T370-Cosworth V8
ret	International Trophy	Silverstone	07/04/74	Embassy Racing	Lola T370-Cosworth V8 *suspension*
ret	**SPANISH GP**	Jarama	28/04/74	Embassy Racing	Lola T370-Cosworth V8 *engine*
8	**BELGIAN GP**	Nivelles	12/05/74	Embassy Racing	Lola T370-Cosworth V8
7	**MONACO GP**	Monte Carlo	26/05/74	Embassy Racing	Lola T370-Cosworth V8
6	**SWEDISH GP**	Anderstorp	09/06/74	Embassy Racing	Lola T370-Cosworth V8
ret	**DUTCH GP**	Zandvoort	23/06/74	Embassy Racing	Lola T370-Cosworth V8 *clutch housing bolts*
13	**FRENCH GP**	Dijon	07/07/74	Embassy Racing	Lola T370-Cosworth V8
13	**BRITISH GP**	Brands Hatch	20/07/74	Embassy Racing	Lola T370-Cosworth V8
9	**GERMAN GP**	Nürburgring	04/08/74	Embassy Racing	Lola T370-Cosworth V8
12	**AUSTRIAN GP**	Österreichring	18/08/74	Embassy Racing	Lola T370-Cosworth V8
8	**ITALIAN GP**	Monza	08/09/74	Embassy Racing	Lola T370-Cosworth V8
14	**CANADIAN GP**	Mosport Park	22/09/74	Embassy Racing	Lola T370-Cosworth V8
8	**US GP**	Watkins Glen	06/10/74	Embassy Racing	Lola T370-Cosworth V8

1975

10	**ARGENTINE GP**	Buenos Aires	12/01/75	Embassy Racing	Lola T370-Cosworth V8
12	**BRAZILIAN GP**	Interlagos	26/01/75	Embassy Racing	Lola T370-Cosworth V8
dns	**SOUTH AFRICAN GP**	Kyalami	01/03/75	Embassy Racing	Lola T370-Cosworth V8 *practice crash*
11	*Daily Express* International Trophy	Silverstone	12/04/75	Embassy Racing	Hill GH1-Cosworth V8
dnq	**MONACO GP**	Monte Carlo	11/05/75	Embassy Racing	Hill GH1-Cosworth V8

Formula 1 World Championship positions/points					
1958	–	–	1967	6th	15
1959	–	–	1968	1st	48
1960	15th	4	1969	7th	19
1961	13th	3	1970	13th	7
1962	1st	(52) 42	1971	21st	2
1963	2nd	29	1972	12th	4
1964	2nd	(39) 41	1973	–	–
1965	2nd	(47) 40	1974	18th	1
1966	5th	17	1975	–	–

Formula 1 World Championship placings 1st–6th + Pole + Fastest lap

1st	2nd	3rd	4th	5th	6th	Pole	Fastest lap	Races
14	15	7	9	7	8	13	10	176

EPILOGUE

Return of a familiar helmet. Damon Hill is following in his late father's footsteps, and has accrued considerable F1 experience in his role as official test driver for Williams.

For all his achievements in a racing car, Bette Hill often refers to her late husband as the 'forgotten champion'. When groups of enthusiasts gather together to discuss the sport's true greats, the names of Moss, Fangio, Clark, Stewart, Prost and Senna dominate the conversation. Hill? He nary merits consideration.

Yet, on his day, Hill could run with, and sometimes ahead of, Clark; the difference between the two was that Clark was very much a natural, and could wring the necessary speed from his car at will. Hill had to work much, much harder to obtain the same results. His CV bears tribute to an extraordinary determination to succeed. He was to Clark and Stewart what Nigel Mansell is to Alain Prost and Ayrton Senna.

The other point, of course, is that Hill wasn't simply a *motor racing* personality. He was public property, a Frank Bruno of the 1960s. Though he could be extremely intense when immersed in his racing, his ability to sparkle in front of the TV cameras had made him popular throughout the world. In Britain, he was a household name, regarded with genuine affection wherever he went.

His wide circle of social contacts was reflected at his funeral, conducted by Robert Runcie, later Archbishop of Canterbury, at St Albans Abbey, where familiar faces from showbusiness and other sports mingled with grieving motor sporting folk.

The Hill GH2 never raced, and now resides in the Donington Collection, alongside the Donington Park circuit in Leicestershire. It has been driven since 1975, however, though only in a private test session.

The young man at the wheel sported a familiar helmet, carrying the colours of the London Rowing Club. Damon Hill, Graham's only son and the second eldest of his three offspring, gave up a successful motor cycle racing career to try his hand at cars in the autumn of 1983. Like his father, he started off at Brands Hatch.

Though the initial venture was unsuccessful, he has since become one of Britain's brightest prospects, winning in Formula Ford and Formula 3 before graduating to Formula 3000, Grand Prix racing's modern ante-chamber. Bette comes along to watch him when she can. 'I don't get too involved, though. In Graham's day, wives and girlfriends were an integral part of the team. Now, they've got computers to do all the timing, and mothers just get in the way!'

At the time of writing, in November 1991, Damon had gainful employment with a top Formula 1 team, in his official capacity as test driver for Williams-Renault.

It may not be long before the colours of the London Rowing Club are carried once again in the sport's highest echelon.